Crazy Horse

Legends of the Wild West

Sitting Bull

Billy the Kid

Calamity Jane

Buffalo Bill Cody

Crazy Horse

Davy Crockett

Wyatt Earp

Geronimo

Wild Bill Hickok

Jesse James

Nat Love

Annie Oakley

Legends of the Wild West

Crazy Horse

Jon Sterngass

CHELSEA HOUSE PUBLISHERS
An imprint of Infobase Publishing

Crazy Horse

Copyright © 2010 by Infobase Publishing

Chelsea House
An imprint of Infobase Publishing
132 West 31st Street
New York NY 10001

Library of Congress Cataloging-in-Publication Data
Sterngass, Jon.
  Crazy Horse / Jon Sterngass.
    p. cm. — (Legends of the Wild West)
  Includes bibliographical references and index.
  ISBN 978-1-60413-526-8 (hardcover)
  1. Crazy Horse, ca. 1842-1877—Juvenile literature. 2. Oglala Indians—Kings and rulers—Biography—Juvenile literature. 3. Indians of North America—Great Plains—Wars—Juvenile literature. I. Title. II. Series.

  E99.O3C729435 2010
  978.004'9752—dc22
  [B   2010006596

Chelsea House books are available at special discounts when purchased in bulk quantities for businesses, associations, institutions, or sales promotions. Please call our Special Sales Department in New York at (212) 967-8800 or (800) 322-8755.

You can find Chelsea House on the World Wide Web at
http://www.chelseahouse.com

Text design by Kerry Casey
Cover design by Keith Trego
Composition by EJB Publishing Services
Cover printed by Bang Printing, Brainerd, Minn.
Book printed and bound by Bang Printing, Brainerd, Minn.
Date printed: August 2010
Printed in the United States of America

10 9 8 7 6 5 4 3 2 1

This book is printed on acid-free paper.

All links and Web addresses were checked and verified to be correct at the time of publication. Because of the dynamic nature of the Web, some addresses and links may have changed since publication and may no longer be valid.

CONTENTS

THE MYSTERIOUS WARRIOR

Deep in the heart of the Black Hills of South Dakota, the Crazy Horse Memorial rises out of Thunderhead Mountain. Under construction since 1948, it is a dramatic monument in the form of Crazy Horse, a Lakota Sioux warrior, riding a horse and pointing into the distance. If completed, the sculpture's final dimensions will be 641 feet (195 meters) wide and 563 feet (172 m) high, making it the world's largest statue. The memorial to Crazy Horse will dwarf one of the most popular monuments in the country, Mount Rushmore, located only eight miles (12 km) away. The heads of the presidents at Mount Rushmore are each 60 feet (18 m) high, but the head of Crazy Horse will be 87 feet (26.5 m) high.

Some wonder, however, if it will ever be finished. The carving was inspired by a letter to sculptor Korczak Ziolkowski, who had worked for a short time on Mount Rushmore. In 1939, Chief Henry Standing Bear wrote to Ziolkowski, "My fellow chiefs and I would like the white man to know that the red man has great heroes, too." Ziolkowski began carving in 1948, and the work has been going on ever since. Ziolkowski died in 1982, but his wife and several children remain closely involved with the work. Although the face of

The Crazy Horse Memorial, located in the Black Hills of South Dakota, is being carved out of Thunderhead Mountain. It has been under construction since 1948. If finished, it will be the world's largest sculpture.

Crazy Horse was completed and dedicated in 1998, the entire work is far from completion.

Yet the monument to Crazy Horse is not without its critics, many of them Lakota. It is being carved out of land considered sacred by some Native Americans. Lame Deer, a Lakota medicine man, remarked, "The whole idea of making a beautiful wild mountain into a statue of him is a pollution of the landscape. It is against the spirit of Crazy Horse." Russell Means, a famous Native American activist, also criticized the creation of the sculpture. Crazy Horse's "story continues to relegate us as a people to the eighteenth and nineteenth centuries," said Means. "People think 'Indian people are relics'; we do not exist in the present. That makes it easy for non-Indians to say, 'Oh, lo, the poor Indian, and we love his romantic image, and we are sorry for what our ancestors did to him, but we can continue to do it to these Indian people today with impunity.'"

So even in death, Crazy Horse continues to inspire people and excite argument. Who was this Lakota warrior and why does he still capture the imagination of twenty-first century America?

A MYSTERIOUS WARRIOR

Crazy Horse is one of the greatest of Native American heroes, but much about his life is a mystery. It is not easy to write his biography. Crazy Horse was quiet and shy. He rarely spoke in public or participated in public ceremonies. He almost never took part in councils, treaty sessions, or any kind of meetings with whites or Native Americans. He was a feared and respected warrior, but he did not brag about his war deeds. He did not leave behind any letters, diaries, speeches, or account books to tell his side of the story. The longest recorded statement by him is barely 200 words.

For almost his whole life, Crazy Horse avoided whites. He lived the life of a Lakota warrior, raiding and hunting on the Northern Plains. For about the first 35 years of his life, it is difficult to determine what he said or felt. His biography can only be assembled from the memories and oral tradition of the Lakota people. Truth telling and the oral historical tradition are important in Native American cultures. Storytellers had fantastic memories for remembering minute details. Yet many times, they related their stories of Crazy Horse 25 to 50 years after the events they described. Their descriptions and recollections are crucial, but they are not always accurate. Sometimes, reliable Native American eyewitnesses even contradict each other.

The mid-nineteenth-century Lakota, like most preindustrial people, were not obsessed with dates and statistics. It is almost impossible to determine the year of Crazy Horse's birth. The chronology of the events of his life is often jumbled. People have told some stories so many times that the stories have acquired the exaggerations of legend. Without anyone to contradict them, people have felt free to add or change details.

In the last two years of his life, Crazy Horse led the Lakota in two of the most famous battles of the American West: the Rosebud and the Little Bighorn. From this period, a great deal of white and Native American documentation exists; however, the U.S. Army recollections and memoirs often are colored by the cultural assumptions and the racism of the time. Army reports sometimes covered up embarrassing incidents or arguments and often tried to glorify minor engagements into victories or explain away defeats.

Native American testimony from these years, while less biased, is also not reliable. Lakota and Cheyenne warriors worried about white revenge and often deliberately distorted the truth. Plains Indians, accounts of battles were usually centered on individuals. They are useful in recalling personal incidents, but they seldom have much to say about group behavior in warfare. There are also problems in the translation of words and phrases.

In the final four months of Crazy Horse's life, he lived on a reservation. For this period, there are almost too many witnesses. American and Lakota sources all seem to have an argument to make, a side to take, or a position to prove. Stories contradict each other, culminating in Crazy Horse's incredibly controversial death. Historians are unable even to agree whether his death was murder or an accident, a planned conspiracy or a huge mistake. The wealth of material means that most biographies of Crazy Horse spend more than half of their pages on the last two years of his life, from the Battle of the Rosebud to his death.

WHERE MY DEAD LIE BURIED

Despite the problems with the sources, Crazy Horse was consistent throughout most of his life. From youth, he associated with those Lakota who rejected negotiations with the United States. As the buffalo herds shrank, many Lakota accepted the inevitable and settled on agencies and reservations supposedly guaranteed by treaty. There, they would be fed by government-issued rations and educated in the ways of the white world.

Until the last four months of his life, Crazy Horse completely rejected the reservation system. John Bourke, who fought against him, noted in *On the Border with Crook*, "Crazy Horse was one of the great soldiers of his day and generation; he never could be friends of the whites, because he was too bold and warlike in his nature...." Crazy Horse, along with Sitting Bull, came to symbolize Lakota military defiance.

Yet Crazy Horse was loved by his own people as much for his charity as for his courage. His generosity with the buffalo he hunted and killed earned him the praise of everyone in the tribe. His modesty was noteworthy in a society that emphasized boasting. He kept no battle spoils except weapons; he distributed food, horses, and other booty to the old and the poor.

Crazy Horse was a victim of bad timing. In 1840, around the time he was born, the Great Plains west of the Mississippi River was Indian country to belong forever to Native Americans. He watched as the Lakota people dwindled because of war and disease. The buffalo died and railroads and fences appeared on the Plains. Whenever Lakota rights conflicted with the land hunger of American settlers, ranchers, mining companies, and railroads, the tribes came out second best. The Lakota Indians repeatedly found themselves cheated and betrayed. By the time of Crazy Horse's death in 1877, there was no longer a free tribe or a "wild" Native American in all the Great Plains, from Canada to Texas. In 37 years, the U.S. government had broken every solemn treaty and promise.

Yet, in an odd sense, Crazy Horse's death was perfectly timed. He fought brilliantly in 1876 at the last great battles at the Rosebud and the Little Bighorn. He became a symbol of Lakota freedom, courage, and dignity. Then he was killed at the exact moment when the old life ways of the Plains Indians also died. By a strange twist of fate, Crazy Horse and the way of life died together. Unlike Geronimo or Red Cloud, he did not live to face the great change, and his reputation was never sullied by imprisonment or compromise.

So, for the Lakota people, and for many Americans, Crazy Horse remains a compelling symbol of resistance. Yet almost nothing remains of him besides the stories. No existing artifact can definitely be said to belong to him. There is no long record of profound pronouncements. There is no grave to visit because his parents deliberately refused to tell anyone where he was buried. There are no

This picture shows a model of the planned sculpture. Because Crazy Horse refused to be photographed, the monument serves as a symbolic tribute to the spirit of the Lakota warrior and leader.

accurate images of him because he never sat for a portrait or allowed himself to be photographed. When the doctor who treated his wife tried to take a picture, Crazy Horse told him, "My friend, why should you wish to shorten my life by taking from me my shadow?"

The lack of an image was an obvious problem when Korczak Ziolkowski began creating his Crazy Horse Monument, but Ziolkowski never thought of his sculpture as a realistic portrait. Instead, he meant it as a symbolic tribute to the spirit of Crazy Horse, the Lakota, and to all Native Americans. "My lands are where my dead lie buried," Crazy Horse supposedly said. In the sculpture, Crazy Horse will point into the distance to the lands that he loved and fought to defend. In a short lifetime, Crazy Horse stamped his personality on the Great Plains and American history. Black Elk, a Lakota warrior and medicine man, concluded, "It does not matter where his body lies, for it is grass; but where his spirit is, it will be good."

GROWING UP ON THE PLAINS

Crazy Horse was born sometime between 1838 and 1842. As far as can be determined, his birthplace was by the Belle Fourche River, near Bear Butte, in what is now South Dakota. When he was born, his parents named him Curly (for his hair). As a teenager he was called His Horses Looking, but when he became a man he was called Crazy Horse.

In Lakota society, a warrior did not usually acquire his permanent name until he had done something to earn it. Crazy Horse's father was also called Crazy Horse. When his son proved that he was courageous in battle, the father transferred the name to his son. After that time, Crazy Horse's father took the name of Worm. (In this book, their "final" names are used throughout to avoid confusion.)

Crazy Horse was not born into one of the great warrior families of the Lakota. Worm was a respected healer, holy man, and interpreter of dreams. Little is known of Crazy Horse's mother. According to one story, his biological mother, Rattle Blanket Woman, committed suicide in 1845. Shortly afterward, Worm remarried Kills Enemy, the daughter of a Minniconjou chief. As time passed, the family grew. Worm took another wife, Iron Between Horns, and Crazy Horse soon had at least two sisters and a brother. Crazy Horse was close to his extended family but he especially loved his younger brother, Young Little Hawk.

According to legend, Crazy Horse was different right from birth. He did not cry when he was born but instead looked at the world with serious eyes. He was a shy boy and often walked or rode into the hills to think alone. Yet even though he seemed different, Crazy Horse had many friends as a child, especially Lone Bear, Horn Chips, and his older mentor, High Backbone (also known as Hump).

Crazy Horse learned the spiritual beliefs of the Lakota from his parents and grandparents. He learned that everything in the world contained a mysterious force that the Lakota called *wakan*. Wakan Tanka, or the "Great Mystery," was a vague omniscient, sky-dwelling creator whose spirit was also present in all things. The Lakota might gain power in several ways, such as through the vision quest or through self-torture at the Sun Dance, a religious ceremony practiced by the Plains Indians that represents life and rebirth.

From an early age, Crazy Horse had a talent with horses. When he grew up, he was good at capturing and breaking wild horses and adept at stealing them from other tribes. For this skill, he acquired the name His Horses Looking, but that name never caught on.

HORSES AND THE GREAT PLAINS

Crazy Horse spent his entire life on the Great Plains, the area between the Mississippi River and the Rocky Mountains extending from Canada to southern Texas. Native American tribes of the Great Plains included the Lakota, Comanche, Kiowa, Arapaho, Blackfoot, Cheyenne, and Crow. Crazy Horse lived on the northern Great Plains, in present-day South Dakota and nearby parts of Wyoming, Nebraska, and North Dakota. It was an area of lush grasslands and cold rivers: the Platte, Niobrara, Powder, Yellowstone, Tongue, and Little Mississippi.

"We did not think of the great open plains, the beautiful rolling hills, and the winding streams with tangled growth, as 'wild,'" said one Native American. "Only to the white man was nature a

Great Plains Culture Area

Otoe Tribe

Note: Map shown with modern boundaries.

0 — 300 miles
0 — 300 km

N

Sarcee

Plains Cree

Blood
Blackfeet

Piegan

Assiniboine Plains Ojibway

Gros Ventre

Lake Superior

Crow

Hidatsa
Mandan

Yanktonai
Sioux
(Nakota)

Arikara

Teton Sioux
(Lakota)

Santee Sioux
(Dakota)

Cheyenne   Ponca

Yankton Sioux
(Nakota)

Omaha

Pawnee

Ioway

Arapaho

Otoe

Kaw

Missouria

Kiowa

Osage

Kiowa-Apache

Quapaw

Comanche

Wichita
Kichai

Tawakoni

Tonkawa

Gulf of Mexico

© Infobase Publishing

During Crazy Horse's time, the Plains Indians lived in a geographical area that ranged from the Mississippi River to the Rocky Mountains and from Canada to Texas. Farming tribes moved onto the Great Plains from river valleys and woodlands to hunt buffalo. Use of the horse revolutionized buffalo hunting, making hunting easier and more productive.

'wilderness' and only to him was the land 'infested' with 'wild' animals and 'savage' people. To us it was tame. Earth was bountiful and we were surrounded with the blessings of the Great Mystery."

Before they acquired horses, Native Americans walked the Plains and used dogs to pull their possessions when they were traveling. They hunted bison on foot, a slow and dangerous activity. They used sticks, bones, horns, and stones for tools. Some people planted crops, and everyone collected seeds and nuts and dug roots.

Life for the Native tribes near the Plains greatly changed when they acquired horses in the mid-1700s. Horses had become extinct in North America about 10,000 years ago, but the Spanish reintroduced them in Mexico in the 1500s, and they slowly passed northward from tribe to tribe. The horse made Native Americans vastly more mobile and increased their ability to follow the buffalo herds. The horse meant the tribes could now ride out on the Plains, erect larger tipis (or teepees), acquire more personal possessions, and live more comfortably. Horses became an important new symbol of individual and tribal wealth.

Horses also turned the Plains Indians into formidable warriors. Warriors traveled farther to trade and raid for them. Stealing horses from an enemy ranked as a major accomplishment. Plains Indians regarded a successful horse thief with almost as much admiration as a brave fighter in battle. Horses were a form of transportation, a medium of trade, a cause of war, a vital weapon of warfare, and, in hard times, even a source of food. Horses became so central to Native American life on the Plains that some tribal legends regarded them as a gift from the gods rather than a result of Europe's invasion of America.

By 1800, the Native Americans who lived on the Great Plains had many cultural traits in common. They were nomadic, hunted large game on horseback, and depended on the buffalo for much of their material culture. They had warrior societies, lived in portable tipis, and went on vision quests. Most practiced some form of the Sun Dance.

Although many Plains Indian tribes practiced the Sun Dance, each tribe had its own distinct ceremonial traditions. It was once outlawed by the U.S. government, but today the Sun Dance is legal and practiced annually on many western reservations. This picture shows a Sun Dance in progress among the Cheyenne in 1910.

THE LAKOTA

The best horsemen of the Plains were the Lakota, known to whites as the Sioux. The Sioux nation was divided roughly into three large groups who spoke a related language. The Dakota lived in the lakes region of Minnesota. Their economy centered on fishing and the harvesting of wild rice. The Nakota lived to the southwest of the Dakotas and were famous for the quarrying of pipestone. The Lakota, the largest group, lived on the prairies and northwestern plains and hunted buffalo.

The Lakota consisted of a loose confederation of seven subgroups: the Oglala, Brulé, Minniconjou, Sans Arc, Blackfoot Lakota, Two Kettles, and Hunkpapa. The Lakota were a proud and aggressive warrior people who used warfare to dominate the Great Plains from 1800 to 1850. The Lakota, however, were not native to the Great Plains. Before 1650, they had lived on the prairies of central Minnesota for hundreds of years. They planted gardens of corn, beans, and squash. They gathered wild rice; hunted deer, elk, and the occasional buffalo; and fished on their ancestral lands.

In the 1700s, the Lakota were pulled west by the horse culture of the Plains. At the same time, they were pushed west by the expansion of the Ojibwa (Chippewa) into Minnesota. The Lakota gave up their farming economy and settled village life. Instead, they became nomadic, establishing temporary camps and following the buffalo herds and other game.

In the time of Crazy Horse, the Lakota roamed across the northern Great Plains. They lived in many loosely related tribes or bands. Each band was usually governed not by a single leader but by councils comprising tribal elders with experience and wisdom.

Crazy Horse was an Oglala. He belonged to the Hunkpatilas, one of seven bands of the Oglala. These divisions, however, were fluid. In his life, Crazy Horse would spend time with many other tribes and groups. At the time of his birth, the Lakota living on the Plains probably numbered no more than 25,000. At the same time, the population of America was about 17 million.

Because the Lakota lived in small groups, they relied on customs, public opinion, and taboos to make sure that all people followed the rules of proper behavior. There was an *akicita*, a warrior society selected to police the village, but ridicule, shame, and gossip usually kept people in line. If members of the community had a disagreement, they could seek advice from the council of elders. Their decisions influenced the community, but they had no power to issue orders.

THE BISON

On the Great Plains, Lakota life revolved around the American bison, also known as the buffalo. These large beasts roamed the prairie in great dark herds that often stretched further than the eye could see. Estimates of buffalo in the United States in 1840 range wildly, from 50 million to more than 100 million. They grazed over the lush grass of the Plains that had never been marked by wagon wheels, divided by fences, or eaten by cattle.

The Lakota depended on the buffalo to meet their most basic material needs. The meat provided food for the entire tribe. If a buffalo herd was nearby, a good buffalo hunter could collect, in a few hours, enough food to feed his family for weeks. The Lakota would eat buffalo meat roasted as well as raw. They cured and dried the leftover meat on racks and cut it into edible strips called jerky. The tougher meat was dried and pounded together with fat and wild berries to make pemmican. Pemmican was a nutritious high-protein food that could easily be carried in a rawhide container called a parfleche and eaten on the trail. If times were bad, Plains Indians ate bison right down to the last bit of marrow.

The bison provided more than just meat. The Lakota were skilled at tanning buffalo hides to soften them. This helped them to make durable leather for moccasins, leggings, shirts, gloves, jackets, vests, and dresses. Thicker buffalo skins served as blankets and robes for the cold winter months. Mothers wrapped Lakota infants in the soft skin of young buffalo calves and, at the other end of life, buffalo hides were used as shrouds for the dead in burial ceremonies.

Buffalo rawhide was also useful in making tools, drums, rattles, and battle shields. Knives and arrowheads were fashioned from bones and horns. The Lakota used the buffalo's stomach as a water container; buffalo hair provided padding, ropes, and ornaments. Buffalo sinew was used for thread, bindings, and bows. Even the hooves could be boiled down for glue. A handy switch or hair ornament could be made from the tail, and dried dung was used to start a fire.

Lakota women sewed together 12 or more buffalo hides as coverings for waterproof tents, which they called lodges or tipis. A tipi was sturdy enough to withstand the harsh winds of the Great Plains, yet light enough to disassemble in minutes. The Lakota often painted their tipi coverings with scenes from their daily life.

For the Lakota, killing buffalo involved some danger and difficulty. Hunters on horses tried to herd the buffalo into a circle. The horses quickly darted in and out of the herds while the warriors guided them with their knees. Even after the Plains Indians acquired guns in the mid-1700s, they continued to use bows and arrows or spears to hunt buffalo. Rifles were heavy to carry and too slow to reload.

Lakota Language

The Lakota had no written language before their contact with Europeans. Instead, they used a writing system based on pictographs. In pictographic writing, a drawing represents exactly what it means; a drawing of a dog literally meant a dog. Native Americans on the Plains also adopted a universal sign language that was extremely helpful for intertribal use.

Lakota was not a written language until Christian missionaries invented the first Lakota alphabet in 1834. They based their spelling system on the Santee (Dakota) dialect and used it to translate the Bible. Since then, there have been several different versions of the Lakota written language. This multitude of different written systems has caused some confusion and conflict among the modern Lakota.

In the late 1800s, Americans made organized attempts to eliminate the Lakota language and replace it with English. The famous Carlisle (Pennsylvania) Indian School strictly prohibited the use of Native languages. These attempts at cultural genocide did not succeed. As of 2009, about 25,000 people spoke the Lakota language. It is the fifth-most spoken Native language in North America, behind Navajo, Cree, Inuit, and Ojibwa.

The end of a successful buffalo hunt was a time for celebration at the camp. Those who stayed behind cheered the returning hunters and organized a large feast. The Lakota respected the buffalo. Their culture, independence, and prosperity all depended on it.

As a boy, Crazy Horse learned the skills needed by a Lakota hunter and warrior. He was good at making arrows as well as tracking and bringing down small game. At about age 12, Crazy Horse went on his first big buffalo hunt. This was a crucial step on the path to Lakota manhood. According to one story, he immediately got a calf with one shot of the bow, although it took him four hours to bring down his second buffalo. That night, around the campfire, older men sang the praises of Crazy Horse.

In recent years, the Lakota language has experienced a slight resurgence. For Lakota parents, speaking the language and teaching it to their children is an important way to preserve their heritage. Traditional stories, children's books, and even games have been translated into Lakota.

In the 1800s, translation was a constant problem in interactions between Lakota and Americans. Only a handful of whites ever learned more than a few Lakota words. Mistranslation of Crazy Horse's words into English may have led directly to the problems that led to his death. Here is an excerpt from "Man Rescued by Eagles" by George Bushotter.

Lakota Language	English translation
Eháŋni héčheš oyáte waŋ igláka áyiŋ na waná éthipi yuŋhȟáŋ wičháša waŋ tȟawiču kiŋ hečíya: "Winúȟča, itȟó wayé mní kte ló," eyá. Ečháš toháŋ waglí šni héhan éna thí po," eyá.	Long ago, the tribe was moving camp and were erecting their tipis at the new place when a man said to his wife: "Wife, I think I must go out and hunt." So don't move on with the tribe if they should go on, but stay camped here until I return."

A WARRIOR'S LIFE

Plains Indians societies were organized around warfare and the hunt. For the Lakota, war was a sacred activity that demanded ritual preparation and supernatural help. They fought for many reasons: to defend themselves, guard hunting grounds, obtain horses, earn glory, and satisfy revenge.

The Lakota considered almost all other Plains tribes their enemies, especially the Pawnee, the Crow, and the Arikara. Their only steady allies were the Cheyenne and the Arapaho. Intertribal warfare, however, resembled a very violent sport more than all-out war. The two opposing sides would face off. There would be lots of shouting, verbal sparring, fake attacks, and dashes. After some individual acts of bravery had been performed and witnessed, everyone yelled a few more times and went home. Now and then, an injury or death would require a later raid for revenge.

The main object of Lakota warriors in battle was to win personal honor and glory, not to destroy the enemy or inflict casualties. Plains Indians did fight some serious battles, but these were rare. Tribes usually withdrew if too many warriors were killed; no tribe wanted to lose valuable manpower. When two tribes fought each other, they usually observed the same unspoken rule: The most successful war party was one that returned with war honors and without casualties.

Most Plains Indians, including the Lakota, judged the actions of warriors in raids or wars based on complex rules of bravery called "counting coup." In this system, the tribe ranked various actions based on the element of danger faced by the warrior. The most prestigious act was to directly risk injury or death by approaching an enemy, attacking or even touching him at close range, and then getting away safely. Lakota warriors believed this was more honorable than shooting someone from a distance. Men acquired status by exhibiting bravery in warfare, scalping their enemies, and stealing their horses. Intertribal warfare also served as the culturally accepted way that young Lakota men showed their bravery.

Plains Indian women participated in the warrior cultures of their societies. They raised their sons to be warriors, celebrated their husbands' achievements in war, and took part in victory dances. As one woman noted, however, "We women did not like war, and yet we could not help it, because our men loved war . . . there was always some woman, sometimes many women, mourning for men who had been killed in war."

Crazy Horse would see warriors returning from raids amid the proud songs of the women, driving in horses and waving enemy scalps. "When we were young," Crazy Horse's friend Horn Chips later said, "all we thought about was going to war with some other nations; all tried to get their names up to the highest, and whoever did so was the principal man of the nation; and [Crazy Horse] wanted to get to the highest rank or station."

Young men began to join war parties soon after their first buffalo hunt. At first, they tagged behind the adults. To become a warrior, a young boy had to go on several raids with an experienced man as an apprentice. The young boys had relatively safe duties such as tending the packhorses and equipment, standing guard, and cooking the food. In June 1855, Crazy Horse went with Spotted Tail in a raid against the Omaha. The two tribes met each other on Beaver Creek. This was Crazy Horse's first battle and, surprisingly, the fighting was heavy. The Lakota killed the chief of the Omaha, and Crazy Horse was on his way to becoming a full-fledged member of Lakota warrior culture.

THE AMERICANS APPEAR

As a young man, Crazy Horse lived many months and even years raiding and hunting in the old Lakota way. This way of life, however, was dying even when he was a boy. French and British traders had entered the Great Plains as early as the 1700s. The pace of contact quickened when whites began taking the Oregon Trail across Lakota lands in the 1840s. Even though the Americans usually did not settle on the Plains at this time, their presence began to affect Native American patterns.

Increased trade with whites led to changes in Lakota lifeways. Whites brought many things that Native tribes of the Plains could use: metal tools, utensils, knives, needles, kettles, scissors, and arrowheads. Native Americans traded buffalo meat and bison robes for bread, coffee, sugar, and liquor. Though it was often illegal, traders sometimes sold them guns and ammunition. Lewis Henry Morgan, a sympathetic observer, traveled up the Missouri River and noted that the Lakota "hate the whites and say that they would clear their country of them if the white man had not become necessary to them. They want his guns, his powder and ball, coffee, blankets, and camp furniture, which have now become indispensable, and they therefore submit to his presence among them."

The predecessor to the modern department store, the general store in the Old West carried all types of goods, from guns and ammunition to lanterns and saddles. Above is a replica of a mid-nineteenth-century general store stocked with fine china, fabrics, and metal household goods, made available for trade with Plains Indians.

The Lakota were a very adaptable people. They preferred to trade for metal goods rather than to spend long hours making tools from stone and wood as they used to do. The need to trade, however, meant that Lakota men had to spend more time and energy killing buffalo. Women had to spend more time processing buffalo meat and tanning buffalo hides for market. By the 1840s, Plains Indians were probably killing more than 300,000 bison a year. "We have long since noticed the decrease of the buffalo," said a Cheyenne chief in 1846, "and we are well aware it cannot last much longer." The herds were still large but they were not quite as easy to find as a generation before. The decline of the bison, though not as great as the later wholesale slaughter by whites, still created conflict. Native tribes fought continuously over the remaining animals and hunting grounds.

White people also brought other problems, including whiskey, which killed and demoralized more Native Americans than the most murderous American soldier. The Lakota had missed the worst of the smallpox and measles epidemics, but they were not immune. In 1849, 20,000 prospectors passed the Platte River valley on their way to the California gold fields. For weeks, their wagon trains crossed Lakota land, destroying pasture, scaring away game, and infecting Native Americans with cholera. Several of Crazy Horse's stepsisters died in this period from smallpox, cholera, or measles.

As a child, Crazy Horse learned to hit a moving target with an arrow and played "buffalo hunt" with his friends; however, that world was fast disappearing. As Crazy Horse became a teenager, the most pressing issue for his people was how to deal with the ever-increasing number of whites passing through Lakota territory.

MANIFEST DESTINY

"Manifest destiny" was the belief among American whites that the expansion of the United States was inevitable, just, and an obligation placed upon Americans by God. The phrase describes a general mood rather than a precise policy, because the limits to this expansion were never officially set. Rapid population growth and advances in transportation, communication, and industry convinced many nineteenth-century Americans that they possessed a unique civilization. The U.S. population had nearly doubled from 1820 to 1840; a growing nation claimed to need ever-more room. Americans believed that democratic institutions and local self-government (at least for white people) would follow the flag.

The fierce national pride of the American people was also self-serving and racist. Americans preferred to justify their invasion and conquest of the West as an attempt to extend liberty and progress rather than a selfish desire for land and economic gain. Believers in manifest destiny proclaimed that only white Americans, whom they felt were among the foremost people in the world, had the energy, industriousness, and love of liberty to establish democratic governments. This explained why so-called inferior groups, such as Catholic Mexicans and "savage" Native Americans, had to be pushed aside, eliminated, or crushed. In the mid-1800s, Americans debated whether the nation's manifest destiny justified the use of force to bring the benefits of American civilization to the world. The right of the United States to expand, however, was almost never debated at all.

Nineteenth-century white Americans believed that the white race had a destiny and the "red race" had only a fate. This line of reasoning presented only two solutions to the "Indian problem": assimilation or extinction. Yet if the Lakota did not choose assimilation, how could extinction take place unless someone did the killing? Most Westerners agreed and consistently supported the extermination of Native Americans. Easterners could afford to be more generous; they had already done their exterminating in previous centuries.

THE FIRST TREATY OF FORT LARAMIE

The main practical problem with manifest destiny was that indigenous peoples already lived on the land that Americans wanted. White Americans had moved thousands of these Native Americans there from the lands east of the Mississippi River from 1820 to 1845. At that time, the United States had told Native Americans that the lands west of the Mississippi would be a safe haven for them for the imaginable future. Now, the tribes stood right in the middle of white migration to the Pacific coast. Native Americans who had initially been friendly to whites found their patience running out. The whites had never had any patience in the first place. They wanted the indigenous peoples' land for farming, grazing, and mining and were determined to do whatever they had to in order to get it.

After the California Gold Rush of 1849, the clash between whites and Native Americans threatened to become a crisis. To prevent open warfare, the U.S. Bureau of Indian Affairs organized a great meeting of the Plains tribes in September 1851. This gathering at Fort Laramie on the Platte River may have attracted as many as 10,000 Native Americans, mostly Lakota. It was probably the greatest assembling of Plains peoples before the gathering near the Little Bighorn River in 1876. There is no direct evidence that young Crazy Horse and his family were at the council; however, it would seem likely that they were present there since it was such an important political and social event.

Twenty-one leaders from eight Native tribes signed the First Treaty of Fort Laramie in 1851. In this treaty, the major tribes on the northern Great Plains agreed to American proposals that they stop raiding each other and recognize and respect tribal boundaries. In the division of the country, the Lakota received the area north of the Platte and west of the Missouri. They pledged that their warriors would not attack travelers, freight wagons, or mail stages crossing their territory along the Oregon Trail.

In exchange for accepting limits on their movements and for the loss of game, the U.S. government agreed to pay the tribes an annual compensation of $50,000 each year for 50 years (later reduced by the U.S. Senate to 10 years). Then, the Americans gave away blankets, kettles, knives, tobacco, and cloth. It was such a bonanza that the Lakota remembered 1851–1852 as the Year of the Big Giveaway.

The Lakota believed the treaty confirmed their dominant power on the Great Plains. One Lakota told an American that the lands south of the Platte River had "once belonged to the Kiowas and the Crows but we whipped those nations out of them, and in this we did what the white men do when they want the lands of the Indian."

However, the Treaty of Fort Laramie only temporarily put off war between the United States and the Native Americans. Rivalry among tribes was one problem. Eventually, the Blackfoot raided the Crow, who of course had to retaliate. The Lakota then attacked the Snake, and the first condition of the treaty disappeared under long-standing Plains Indian tradition. The larger problem, however, was constant American expansion into Native territory. An estimated 60,000 whites made their way west in 1852, and another 45,000 made the journey in 1853–1854. The trails were crowded, and the pressure on Lakota land was enormous.

THE FIRST LAKOTA WAR

To many Lakota, stealing and harassment were games, a test of their warrior skills. Americans on the Oregon Trail viewed this behavior differently. The whites complained to the commander at Fort Laramie about many such Native American incidents.

This would have tragic repercussions in August 1854. A misunderstanding over the loss of an emigrant's cow led Lieutenant John Grattan and 30 men to enter the Lakota camp near Fort Laramie. The brash and boastful Grattan hated Native Americans and foolishly refused to negotiate a settlement. Instead, he insisted on arresting the man who stole the cow. Tension mounted, and the discussion turned to an argument. A Brulé chief was shot and killed as he tried to keep the situation from escalating, and a riot broke out. The Lakota surrounded and killed all of Grattan's greatly outnumbered men.

Some army officers and even the U.S. government condemned Grattan's provocative actions. Military officers, however, did not want the Grattan Fight to go unpunished for fear it would send the wrong message to the Lakota. In the summer of 1855, Indian agent Thomas Twiss ordered all Native Americans to stay south of the Platte River, where he promised they would be protected and receive the goods guaranteed by the 1851 treaty. Any Native Americans who chose to stay north of the Platte would be considered hostile and have to face American soldiers.

In September 1855, General William Harney launched an expedition on the Oregon Trail, looking for some Native Americans to kill. His large force of 600 men found the village of Little Thunder, a Brulé leader camped on the Bluewater River in western Nebraska. Little Thunder knew Harney was coming but felt he had nothing to fear, so the village took no defensive measures. Little Thunder was a friendly chief, although some of his people may have been involved in raiding Americans.

That was enough reason for Harney to attack the village without warning from two directions. Out of about 250 people, almost half were killed or captured. Harney's men mowed down any Lakota who did not run away fast enough; most of the dead were women and children. Harney later admitted he had attacked a friendly village, and afterward the Lakota called him "The Butcher." However, Harney's "victory" in the so-called Battle of Blue Water Creek led to a fragile peace on the northern Plains for about 10 years. The United States now controlled the Platte River and the Oregon Trail, and Harney imposed humiliating terms on the Lakota chiefs.

Crazy Horse would have been about 15 at the time of these events. He was too young to be a warrior but old enough to take an interest. The teenaged Crazy Horse might have been present at the Grattan Fight. His family may have been camping next to the Oregon Trail a few miles east of Fort Laramie. It is even possible that Crazy Horse was living with Little Thunder in the summer of 1855 but was out hunting when the terrible attack came. There is a tendency, however, to place Crazy Horse at the scene of every incident and battle on the northern Great Plains. He may have seen the Grattan Fight or the Battle of Blue Water Creek, but there is no evidence and it is impossible to know for sure.

CRAZY HORSE'S POWER

Sometime around 1854 (some sources say 1860), Crazy Horse rode off alone to seek a vision. Perhaps the increasing friction between whites and the Lakota people troubled him. Perhaps he just felt the need for strength and advice. Vision quests were common among almost all the Plains tribes. They were a way for members of the tribe to seek knowledge. A successful vision quest produced a contact with a guide who could help solve a problem, provide a spirit helper, or possibly even reveal the future. The Lakota believed that mysterious powers existed in all things, including animals, plants, rocks, and the earth. The key to life was somehow to tap into that power. A personal vision was a way to do that.

Crazy Horse often tried to communicate with this mysterious world. His most famous vision has been described in various ways, but it has become an essential element in the legend of Crazy Horse.

Crazy Horse "dreamed" of a man on a horse that floated above the ground. The rider was dressed plainly without paint. The horse may have been dancing; it seemed in some way to be magical. A red-backed hawk flew above the man's head. The man on the horse told Crazy Horse not to dress in a fancy manner. He was told not to wear

Scalping and Torture

Scalping is the removal of all or part of the scalp, usually with hair attached, from an enemy's head. Scalps might be displayed as proof of bravery. The Lakota took body parts as trophies long before they met Europeans. Scalping, however, was also practiced in other parts of the world, from prehistory right into the twenty-first century. Victors in every culture have mutilated the bodies of their dead enemies as a sign of anger, madness, frustration, superiority, hatred, or just plain meanness.

The Lakota dreaded being scalped by their enemies. They believed mutilated victims would remain scarred and humiliated forever in The Happy Place (heaven). Americans also feared scalping; to them it represented the undisciplined savagery of Native Americans. Ironically, white governments frequently encouraged the practice by offering a bounty on Natives' scalps.

By the nineteenth century, scalping of the dead was a tradition on the Great Plains, as Native Americans and whites committed atrocities on the bodies of their dead enemies. Sensationalized incidents of the mutilation of Americans occurred after the Fetterman Fight and the Battle of the Little Bighorn, while whites famously abused corpses after the Sand Creek Massacre. It is probably impossible to determine who learned scalping from whom. There was plenty of blame to go around. Both sides considered its own actions justified and their opponents provocative and murderous. This was a recipe for atrocity. Scalping, however, became associated with Native Americans even though white Americans practiced it as much or more than the Native tribes. It was a basic part of American propaganda to demonize the Native American.

a war bonnet but only a single feather. Crazy Horse was instructed to throw a little dust over his horse before going into battle and to wear a small stone behind his ear. In the vision, there may have been a battle but neither bullets nor arrows touched him. The horseman told Crazy Horse never to keep anything for himself.

It seems that Crazy Horse tried his best to follow his vision. If he used war paint, it was only a zigzag representing lightning and a few white spots representing hail or snow. People reported that Crazy Horse threw dust on himself and his horse before going into battle, wore a single feather, and put a small stone behind his ear. He never wore an eagle feather headdress or bragged about his accomplishments. All his life, the Lakota admired his generosity and lack of concern for material possessions. He always did his best to feed the poor and helpless members of his tribe.

One other part of Crazy Horse's vision has become legendary. In one retelling of the dream, the horseman had his arms held by one of his own people in the battle. This was interpreted to mean that Crazy Horse could be injured only if one of his own people held his arms. On two crucial occasions, a Lakota may have held Crazy Horse's arms and he was seriously injured.

After experiencing this vision, Crazy Horse followed the custom of creating a sacred (medicine) bundle. In the bundle, he placed objects, fetishes, charms, and other physical symbols that he had been directed to collect during the vision. The bundle was made from the skin of a hawk, and its contents reminded Crazy Horse of his mystical powers. The bundle became Crazy Horse's protective war charm. In times of crisis, he would open the bundle, sing certain songs, and pray to the powers in the sacred items. He came to regard the hawk, a symbol of swiftness and endurance, as his personal spiritual protector. Throughout his life, he would invoke the aid of the hawk.

"Crazy Horse put great confidence in his medicine," Horn Chips said. "He seemed to bear a charmed life, and no matter how near he got to his enemy they could not hit him." Black Elk agreed: "It was this vision that gave him his great power, for when he went into a fight, he had only to think of that world to be in it again, so that he could go through anything and not be hurt. . . ."

THE GREAT LAKOTA COUNCIL OF 1857

In May 1857, the teenaged Crazy Horse took part in a raid against the Pawnee, in which he made a dramatic horseback charge, surpassing even veteran Lakota warriors. The following fight, he counted coup several times. "From that time on," remembered Eagle Elk, "he was talked about."

That summer, Crazy Horse rode south with some Cheyenne friends. He almost certainly took part in the Cheyenne's famous encounter with Colonel Edwin Sumner. The Cheyenne had convinced themselves that they had sacred power that could make the army's guns powerless. On July 29, 1857, about 300 cavalrymen under Sumner met an equal number of Cheyenne warriors in the Battle of Solomon Fork in western Kansas. Just as the overconfident Cheyenne warriors were about to attack, an amazing thing happened. In an unexpected move, Sumner ordered his soldiers to make a saber charge. No one knows why he gave the order; it was probably the only full-fledged saber charge ever made on the Plains. The stunned Cheyenne warriors fled in astonishment, their anti-bullet magic completely negated. It wasn't much of a battle—the Cheyenne suffered four killed and the Americans two—but it probably helped convince Crazy Horse to avoid fighting the U.S. Army in a pitched battle if possible.

Crazy Horse returned to his people in 1857 in time for the Great Council near Bear Butte in the Black Hills. With the exception of Spotted Tail, all the great Lakota chiefs were there, including Sitting Bull from the Hunkpapas, Lone Horn from the Minniconjou, and Old Man Afraid of His Horse and Red Cloud from the Oglala. Young Crazy Horse was there too, along with his older friend Hump and the extremely tall Minniconjou known as Touch the Clouds. The leaders agreed that they needed to take a tougher line before the whites destroyed their hunting grounds and took over all their lands. At the Bear Butte council, according to Bear Ribs, "they agreed together to hereafter let no one come." Later that fall, Lakota warriors forcibly prevented a U.S. Army survey party from crossing the Black Hills.

The Great Council at Bear Butte changed very little, however. A united Lakota policy was almost impossible to enforce. Each band followed the game and looked out for its own needs. The whites had a great advantage; they were one nation while the Native peoples of the Great Plains were many nations.

In 1861, however, the whites split into two nations themselves and fought a huge civil war. The Civil War was so bloody that it made the conflicts with the Plains Indians seem like frolics. The U.S. Army transferred its best officers to fight in the Civil War, leaving the western forts undermanned by resentful officers and soldiers.

CRAZY HORSE EARNS HIS NAME

As with most of Crazy Horse's life, there are conflicting accounts about how, when, and against whom Crazy Horse exhibited the bravery that prompted his father to pass on the family name. In September 1857 (or any year from 1858 to 1862, depending on the source), Crazy Horse accompanied several warriors on a war party against the Arapaho. Crazy Horse was in the thick of the battle, but he managed to avoid the bullets and arrows that flew close to him. His bravery was so exceptional that the Lakota began to sing in his honor.

He Dog said, "Although [Crazy Horse] was just a boy, he charged them several times alone and came back wounded but with two Arapaho scalps." He also may have counted coup on a fallen Arapaho warrior whom none of the other Lakota warriors had been able to touch. Horn Chips recalled how it seemed that Crazy Horse's pony "became unmanageable" as he danced and twirled and stuttered his way through the buzzing bullets to the fallen Arapaho. In a single battle, Crazy Horse counted at least five coups.

In his excitement, Crazy Horse jumped from his horse and took two scalps of the warriors he had killed. According to one story, an arrow struck him in the leg as he remounted. The wound was not serious, but it became incorporated in the Crazy Horse legend. Hadn't the man in the vision told him never to take anything for himself? Now he had been punished. Crazy Horse threw the scalps away. In the future, he believed that his medicine would be strong as long as he followed the instructions in his vision.

The war party was a victory for the Lakota; they took many horses, counted coups, and did not lose a man. At the camp circle that night, as was the custom, the warriors told of their brave deeds and heard the listeners' praises. Crazy Horse, who could have boasted about his exploits, merely listened to the others. Some of those who were in the battle, however, told how Crazy Horse had proven himself a brave warrior.

Crazy Horse's father—Crazy Horse, the elder—was proud of his fearless son. He made a fine ceremony, transferred his name to his son, and took the name Worm for himself. By 1860, Crazy Horse was about 20 years old and on his way to becoming a great warrior.

THE WARRIOR

Throughout the late 1850s and early 1860s, Crazy Horse went on almost yearly raids against the Crows, Shoshones, and other western tribes. He fought bravely and became an inspirational war leader. Lakota warriors revered him for his seeming invulnerability, luck, and power. He was always first in a charge, but he fought carefully and rarely with reckless bravery. If Crazy Horse felt a raid might be unsuccessful, he usually turned for home, ignoring the criticism of more impulsive braves. He did not share the suicidal bravery of some of the Lakota warriors.

In those years, Crazy Horse earned the high reputation among his tribe that he would carry with him the rest of his life. Thunder Tail remembered that back in camp after one early fight, "He sat among all the bravest of the young men. They talked very much

The Powder River country of Wyoming and Montana lies between the Bighorn Mountains and the Black Hills. It was a vital hunting ground to the Lakota people. Its location along the Bozeman Trail, an overland route to the Montana gold fields, would lead to war between the Lakota and the United States.

about him." The Lakota people recognized three important types of warrior: a great hunter, a great scout, or a great fighter of battles. Usually a man could master only one of these skills. Crazy Horse, however, excelled at all three.

In one noted battle in the summer of 1861, Crazy Horse led some Cheyenne and Lakota warriors against the village of Washakie, chief of the Snake tribe, on the Sweetwater River. Crazy Horse fought in his unusual style, jumping from his horse before he shot so that his aim would be more accurate. In the long fight, Crazy Horse distinguished himself again by his bravery. The Lakota counted many coup, the raiders stole 400 horses, and they killed the son of Washakie.

Crazy Horse had an awesome reputation among younger warriors. They respected him because he was not greedy for glory after he established his reputation. "He does not count many coups," remembered Eagle Elk. "He is in front and attacks the enemy. If he shoots down an enemy, he does not count coup. He drops behind and lets others count three or four coup counts. He takes the last coup."

The years of Crazy Horse's early manhood were a time of relative prosperity for the Lakota. The tribes followed the game into the rich area between the Black Hills and the Bighorn Mountains and made it their last great hunting ground. In this area, several streams flowed northward to join the Yellowstone. The most important ones were the Rosebud Creek, Tongue River, and Powder River. The Powder River was the longest and had the most tributaries, and for that reason the area was called the Powder River country.

The Powder River country was a beautiful land with many sloping meadows covered with thick grass. Trout-filled streams of clear water flowed through valleys with aspen, willow, and cottonwood. On the mountains, there were forests of pine, fir, and spruce. Buffalo, elk, and antelope grazed on the open grasslands. The animals were abundant and the hunting was easy. The Lakota had conquered most of the Powder River country from the Crow. They did not intend to give it up without a fight.

THE POWDER RIVER WARS

In Minnesota, the Dakota had stayed closer to the land of their ancestors than the Lakota. In the late 1850s, however, the Dakota often did not receive the annuity payments and agricultural aid promised by treaties with the United States. The increasing hunger and hardship angered the Dakota. The U.S. Indian agents were corrupt and stole money and supplies that were supposed to go to the tribe. By 1862, the Dakota had been restricted to a territory 150 miles (241 km) long and just 15 miles (24 km) wide.

In August 1862, when the annuity payment was late, the Dakota rose up and killed more than 400 white settlers in a bloodbath across the prairie. They hoped to take advantage of the Civil War to throw the whites completely out of Minnesota.

President Abraham Lincoln appointed John Pope, the inept commander of Union forces at the Second Battle of Bull Run, to crush the uprising. Pope promised to deal with the Dakota "as maniacs or wild beasts." He said, "It is my purpose to utterly exterminate the Sioux." By 1863, whites had regained the upper hand. Minnesota, the ancient homeland of the Dakota, became exclusively white land.

In early December, a military court convicted 303 Dakota prisoners of murder and rape and sentenced them all to death. Some trials lasted less than five minutes; on the last day alone, the court heard and decided nearly 40 cases. President Lincoln commuted the sentences of most, but he did authorize the hanging of 38. This was the largest mass execution in American history. Those Dakota who escaped fled to their Lakota relatives farther west. Their stories only confirmed the Lakota's worries about white intruders and American intentions.

THE SAND CREEK MASSACRE

The Lakota did not have many reliable allies, but the Cheyenne were most likely to fight with them. The Cheyenne were a much smaller tribe than the Lakota, but they shared the nomadic culture of the Plains based on hunting buffalo. Although the Lakota and Cheyenne occasionally fought each other, they spent much more time fighting the Crow and Pawnee.

In 1851, the First Treaty of Fort Laramie established Cheyenne "territory" in northern Colorado. In 1864, however, the discovery of gold there led to an influx of whites. The territorial government proclaimed that "friendly Indians" should place themselves under the protection of the military at Fort Lyon. Some of the Cheyenne and Arapaho, under Black Kettle and White Antelope, took up the offer. They believed the tribe was safe because they were following the government's orders and locating their camp within the defined reservation.

They did not reckon on John Chivington, an arrogant religious fanatic with political ambitions who despised Native Americans. On November 29, 1864, in a blinding snowstorm, Chivington led the Colorado militia in attacking the Cheyenne at Sand Creek, where they had gathered under the governor's protection. "We must kill them big and little," Chivington said. The militia obliged and slaughtered at least 150 Cheyenne, more than two-thirds of whom were women and children.

The Sand Creek Massacre remains one of the most shameful incidents in United States history. It fits perfectly the definition of a massacre: the use of complete surprise against people who did not consider themselves at war and in which troops had orders to kill anyone without allowing them the chance to surrender. George Bent, who was in the village, related the following haunting image:

Although John Chivington preached against slavery as a Methodist minister and fought against the Confederates in the Civil War, he despised Native Americans so profoundly he declared that "if any of them [Cheyenne] are caught in your vicinity, the only thing to do is kill them."

"I looked toward the chief's lodge and saw that Black Kettle had a large American flag tied to the end of a long lodge pole and was standing in front of his lodge, holding the pole, with the flag fluttering in the gray light of the winter dawn. I heard him call to the people not to be afraid, that the soldiers would not hurt them; then the troops opened fire from two sides of the camps."

The U.S. Congress condemned Chivington, declaring, "Not content with killing women and children, who were incapable of offering any resistance, the soldiers engaged in acts of barbarity of the most revolting character. . . . No attempt was made by the officers to restrain the savage cruelty of the men." White settlers in Colorado, however, viewed these Easterners as naive do-gooders who did not understand reality. When Americans were in the mood to punish Native Americans, they would attack whichever group they came across. It did not matter to most western whites whether a particular Native American group was hostile or friendly; the white expression of the time was, "The only good Indian is a dead Indian."

Sand Creek was a disaster for the Native peoples who desired peace on the Plains. Those Lakota and Cheyenne who had supported treaty making with the United States now looked foolish. Cheyenne refugees joined the Lakota to bring war to the northern Great Plains. In early 1865, Native Americans ripped up telegraph wire, ambushed emigrant wagon trains, and attacked white settlements.

Crazy Horse participated in several of these raids along the North Platte, striking at trading posts and ranches, harassing settlers, and stealing horses. He had spent some time with the Cheyenne and had close ties to the tribe. After Sand Creek, it did not take much for him to join in raids of vengeance against the Americans. The Lakota warriors also did not always discriminate between the guilty and the innocent when they attacked white settlers.

THE BOZEMAN TRAIL

When whites discovered gold in Montana in the early 1860s, they began traveling on the Bozeman Trail, which passed directly through Native American land specifically reserved by treaty to the

Shoshone, Arapaho, and Lakota nations. The flow of white settlers through the territory of Native Americans naturally provoked their resentment and attacks.

Although known as the Bozeman Trail, the north-south trail had been followed by Native Americans since prehistoric times. The route was also familiar to early nineteenth-century white explorers, trappers, and traders. In 1863, John Bozeman and John Jacobs scouted out the direct route from Virginia City, Montana, to central Wyoming to connect with the Oregon Trail. This route was more direct and better watered than any other way to get to Montana. The two men did not create the Bozeman Trail, but they promoted the route and widened it so wagons could use it.

Only about 3,500 emigrants used the 500-mile (804-km) Bozeman Trail, most traveling in 1864. The reason for its lack of use was that the Lakota west of the Mississippi would not allow it. "The band I was in," recalled one Lakota youth, "got together and said they were not going to let the white man run over them." In a council in 1863, the Lakota for the first time identified the Americans as enemies who had to be stopped, by war if necessary.

Crazy Horse did not make this policy but he wholeheartedly agreed with it. He gladly participated in the large-scale offensive that the Lakota and Cheyenne warriors organized in 1865. On July 25, a massive war party of several hundred warriors attempted to attack the outpost and 1,000-foot- (1,609-km-) long bridge where the Overland Trail crossed the North Platte River at present-day Casper, Wyoming. Despite some success, the large Native force could not draw the whites into a major battle, and the warriors went home disappointed. Crazy Horse may have served as one of the decoys in the attack.

The army responded by sending out the Powder River Expedition, headed by General Patrick Connor, to attack the Plains tribes. Connor encouraged his troops to commit genocide by ordering them, "You will not receive orders of peace or submission from Indians, but will attack and kill every male Indian over twelve years of age." Connor defeated the Arapaho in August 1865 at the Battle of Tongue River (Wyoming), but he was far less effective against the

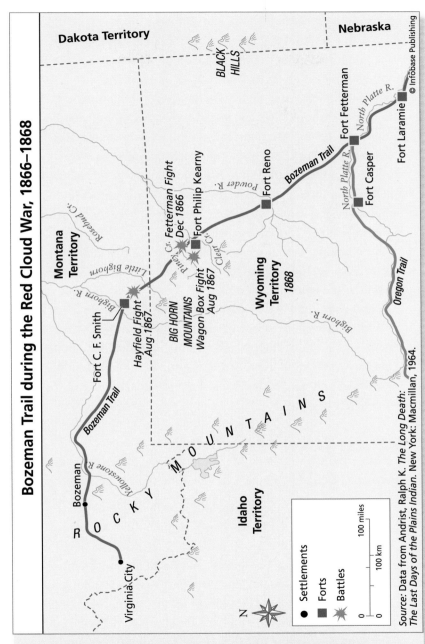

Bozeman Trail during the Red Cloud War, 1866–1868

The opening of the Bozeman Trail through northeast Wyoming and southeast Montana to prospectors searching for gold angered the Native Americans who had traditionally used those lands for hunting. In response to the influx of intruders, Lakota chief Red Cloud led attacks against the non-Indian trespassers.

Cheyenne and Lakota. Crazy Horse fought in several of the skirmishes that frustrated Connor's forces. In one, he supposedly rode back and forth across the U.S. Army lines, well within range of the soldiers' bullets, yet he remained untouched by them.

William Tecumseh Sherman, the Civil War hero who had led the march through Georgia, was the commanding general of the U.S. Army. In 1866, Sherman called for the Lakota to attend a peace conference at Fort Laramie to negotiate permission for whites to use the Bozeman Trail. While the conference was in session, Colonel Henry Carrington arrived with 1,300 men and construction supplies. He freely told the Lakota that Sherman had ordered him to establish military forts along the trail.

The Lakota were understandably shocked that the U.S. peace commission would bargain in such bad faith. Red Cloud, who was present at the council, was outraged. "Great Father sends us presents and wants new road," said Red Cloud, "but White Chief goes with soldiers to steal road before Indian says yes or no." Most of the chiefs stalked out of the council, promising resistance against any whites who sought to use the trail or settle in the area. In July 1866, Crazy Horse began making raids along the Bozeman Trail. The inevitable war had begun.

THE BATTLE OF ONE HUNDRED SLAIN

The U.S. Army built three forts to guard the Bozeman Trail: Fort Reno on the Powder River about 170 miles (273 km) from Fort Laramie; Fort Phil Kearny, 70 miles (112 km) further north (near present-day Sheridan, Wyoming); and Fort C.F. Smith on the Bighorn River. By November, Lakota war parties were attacking wagon trains, and the Americans in the forts became virtual prisoners. The Lakota especially liked to raid the woodcutting and haying details of Fort Phil Kearny; the soldiers counted 51 raids in five months.

Captain William Fetterman was a frustrated young officer stationed at Fort Phil Kearny. It upset him that Colonel Carrington did not seem to want to fight the Lakota. With only about 400 soldiers, Carrington rightly felt it was impossible to march around the countryside searching for Lakota to attack. Fetterman, however, had no regard for the fighting abilities of Native Americans. He supposedly said that with 80 men, he could march through the entire Lakota nation. Unlike Carrington, Fetterman had extensive combat experience during the Civil War, but he had no experience fighting Native Americans.

As winter closed in, the Lakota, Cheyenne, and some Arapaho, led by Hump, worked out a plan. They decided to try the old trick of using decoys to lure the soldiers into a great ambush. The group even rehearsed the ambush so that the young warriors would not spring the trap prematurely. Crazy Horse would be the leader of the 10 decoys.

On December 21, 1866, Fetterman demanded that Carrington allow him to lead some soldiers to defend woodcutters who were being harassed by a few Lakota. Carrington reluctantly consented, but also gave Fetterman explicit orders that he absolutely was not to follow the Lakota over Lodge Trail Ridge, a move that would take Fetterman's men out of sight of the fort.

Crazy Horse's job was to tempt the soldiers over Lodge Trail Ridge, where Carrington had ordered them not to go. According to legend, Crazy Horse skillfully led the soldiers further and further from safety. He dismounted several times and pretended that his horse was lame. At one point, he may have even built a small fire.

Fetterman foolishly took the bait and led his 80 soldiers over the ridge and down the other side—directly into an ambush of some 1,500 warriors. The soldiers had about 3,000 rounds of ammunition, and some fired all they had. At the same time, the Native Americans might have fired as many as 40,000 arrows. At the end of that half hour, Fetterman and all his men were dead; bullets had hit only 4 of the 81. The Lakota suffered only 11 deaths, although one of them was Lone Bear, Crazy Horse's friend.

Once the fighting ended, the Lakota sang the praises of Crazy Horse. They related how Crazy Horse had led the charge into the

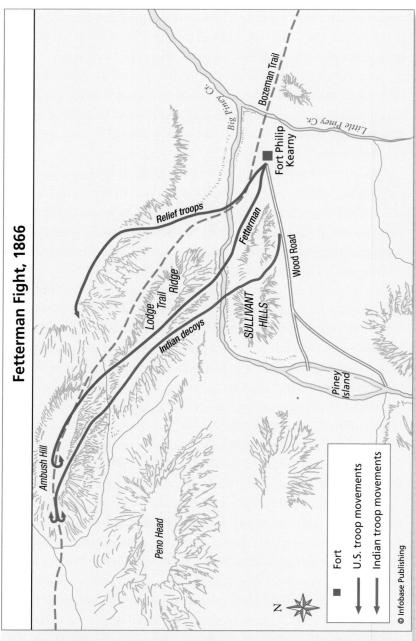

Fetterman Fight, 1866

Captain Fetterman, with only 80 men, set out from Fort Philip Kearny in pursuit of the Lakota. Ignoring orders not to cross Lodge Trail Ridge, Fetterman was lured into a major ambush and all of his men were slaughtered.

cavalry, hacking around him with a hatchet as he rode among the soldiers. After the Fetterman fight, Crazy Horse could never again disappear into anonymity. Chiefs would now consult with him, and his opinion mattered.

Mitch Boyer, a famous scout, explained that the Native Americans killed Fetterman's soldiers because "the whites were building forts in the country and traveling this road, driving off their game, and if they allowed it to go on, in two years they would not have anything for their children to eat." General Sherman, however, advocated genocide as a solution. "I do not understand how the massacre of Colonel Fetterman's party could have been so complete," said Sherman. "We must act with vindictive earnestness against the Lakota, even to their extermination, men, women, and children. Nothing else will reach the root of this case."

LAKOTA FIGHTING

The Lakota warriors sometimes lost battles with the army because they did not fight as one unit. On the battlefield, they behaved as if every warrior was his own general. A fighter attacked when he wanted to attack, retreated when the weather was bad or when he did not like the odds. "A war leader might give orders to fight," said one Hunkpapa, "but he does not direct how to proceed."

Still, the Lakota had several advantages over the Americans. They were formidable warriors and superb horsemen. They knew their homeland thoroughly. They were extremely mobile, lacking wagon trains for supplies and rations. Each warrior could carry dozens of arrows and keep one or more in the air constantly. They were fighting for their families and homeland while their American opponents were just hired soldiers.

The Native tribes of the Great Plains, however, could not win a long fight. They had no factories and very little concept of a united long-term effort. They often seemed more interested in skirmishing with other tribes and stealing horses than in fighting the white invaders. The Lakota warriors had to fight with their families close by. When the U.S. Army later adopted a policy of attacking the Lakota in their winter camps, resistance usually broke down completely. Most battles ended with the Lakota in retreat, even when they had won, for their supplies were exhausted and their ideas about warfare did not include the idea of controlling a strategic location. Despite Crazy Horse's best efforts, war for the Lakota remained a series of individual fights in which counting coup was as important as killing the enemy.

The Lakota also lacked the weaponry of the Americans. Less than 10 percent of the warriors at the Fetterman fight had guns, and most of them were the smoothbore flintlocks of the trading era. In the following decades, the Lakota traded intensively for weapons with anyone who would give them to them. When Crazy Horse finally surrendered in 1876, about half of his warriors had firearms and about one in ten warriors owned a repeater.

Because the American soldiers usually had better weapons, the Lakota used hit-and-run raids by small war parties. This frustrated the army's efforts to concentrate forces against warriors willing to stand and fight. The Lakota tried their best to avoid pitched battles with the infantry, who were less prone to panic than cavalry. The Lakota simply could not match dug-in troops with long-range accurate rifles.

It is hard to determine how much of a tactical sense Crazy Horse developed. Fighting was a huge part of his life and he was in many battles, big and small, so he must have known something. "He didn't like to start a battle," remembered He Dog, "unless he had it all planned out in his head and knew he was going to win. He always used judgment and played it safe." Some historians believe he was a master strategist; others see him as a very daring warrior who inspired others to bravery.

RED CLOUD'S WAR

The war from 1866 to 1868 between the Lakota and the United States was known as Red Cloud's War, after the Oglala war chief. In the summer of 1867, Red Cloud tried to press his advantage against the Americans. After their annual Sun Dance ceremony, bands of

Lakota joined with the Cheyenne to launch a coordinated attack on the Bozeman Trail forts. Approximately 500 Cheyenne and Lakota moved against Fort C.F. Smith, and about 1,500 headed toward Fort

Lakota chief Red Cloud led one of the most important victories against the U.S. military during the Indian wars. Later he was the leader of the Red Cloud Agency, a reservation on the Platte River in Wyoming Territory.

Phil Kearny. These attacks, however, had a different outcome than the Fetterman fight.

Six miles (nine km) from Fort Kearny was a woodcutters camp, where soldiers guarded civilian crews who cut wood for the fort. On August 2, about 1,000 Lakota and Cheyenne warriors under the leadership of Crazy Horse, Hump, and Little Wolf attacked Captain James Powell and 31 soldiers. Powell's men took refuge inside an oval corral formed by laying 14 wagons end to end. They repeatedly turned back Native charges, several led by Crazy Horse. Red Cloud later said that he lost the flower of his men in that fight.

The Lakota suffered heavy losses, possibly as many as 60 warriors killed, compared to only 5 Americans. The unequal casualties were mainly the result of the recent issue of new breech-loading Springfield Model 1866 rifles to the American soldiers. The Springfield 1866 was still a single shot weapon, but the empty cartridge could be ejected and a new one slapped into the breech in a moment. Lakota warriors had always based their attack strategy on the long reloading time of muzzle-loading weapons. When they charged on this day, however, the murderous fire from behind the wagons never ceased. The so-called Wagon Box Fight lasted for about five hours, until a relief force from Fort Phil Kearny finally arrived and the attackers withdrew.

The day before, the other Native American group had struck at Fort C.F. Smith and suffered an almost identical defeat in what is known as the Hayfield Fight. Crazy Horse did not forget these lessons. In subsequent battles, he tried to keep the fighting open and mobile. By keeping the soldiers on the run, Crazy Horse tried to prevent them from creating a secure defensive position. Perhaps just as important, by the early 1870s Crazy Horse owned his own Springfield breechloader.

Despite these setbacks, the Lakota still held the Bozeman Trail and the three forts were completely isolated. Civilian and freight travel along the trail completely ceased, and only well-armed army convoys traveled the road between the forts. The soldiers in the forts often had to fight just to obtain wood and water. Crazy Horse and his

Red Cloud

Red Cloud (1822–1909) was one of the most important Lakota leaders of the nineteenth century. He was about 20 years older than Crazy Horse and had been the greatest Lakota warrior of his generation. Red Cloud had a powerful physical presence, and he was a clever political schemer and a great orator. He was not without his enemies, though; many of the Lakota thought he was a vain windbag.

After his victory in the war named after him, Red Cloud never again took up arms against the United States. He received an agency of his own and became a "reservation chief." This earned him the condemnation of the more militant Lakota. He did not have good relations with Crazy Horse after 1870. In fact, Red Cloud's jealousy and scheming led to Crazy Horse's death in 1877.

Red Cloud, however, continued to work for Lakota rights. He struggled to get honest Indian agents appointed and tried to remind Americans to honor their treaty pledges. In 1870, Red Cloud went to New York and Washington, where he told the U.S. Secretary of the Interior, "When we first had this land we were strong, now are melting like snow on the hillside, while you are grown like spring grass.... When the white man comes in my country, he leaves a trail of blood behind him.

After his trip to the East, Red Cloud decided that Americans were too powerful to oppose directly. He believed that the whites meant to take all of the Lakota's land; the best the Lakota could do was to get the best price or make the best deal. For this reason, Red Cloud tried to use the agency system to win concessions from the U.S. government.

Crazy Horse never parleyed with whites and he never went east. Except for the last four months of his life, he never lived on a reservation. This has helped Crazy Horse's modern reputation as a freedom fighter and symbol of Lakota existence. It also means, however, that Crazy Horse never made the same sort of practical evaluation of American intentions that Red Cloud had to make. Crazy Horse is the more admirable figure, but in many ways Red Cloud was the more realistic.

supporters insisted that they would not negotiate unless the United States abandoned the forts.

THE SECOND TREATY OF FORT LARAMIE

The expense of the fighting shocked many Easterners, and Congress was determined to cut the military budget. Crazy Horse and other Lakota war parties continued raiding along the Bozeman Trail, and the American casualties kept mounting. After the failure of an army offensive against the Lakota in 1867, the U.S. government changed tactics. In 1868, at a series of meetings on the Plains, the two sides hammered out the Second Treaty of Fort Laramie. Red Cloud's War turned out to be the only war in which Native Americans achieved their goals, if only for a brief time.

In the treaty, the United States abandoned the Bozeman Trail and all the military posts in Lakota territory. The government also guaranteed the Lakota permanent ownership of the western half of South Dakota, known as the Great Sioux Reservation. The Powder River country in Wyoming and Montana was reserved "for the absolute and undisturbed use and occupation" of the Lakota. The treaty read, "The United States hereby agrees and stipulates that the country north of the North Platte River and east of the summits of the Bighorn Mountains shall be held and considered to be unceded Indian territory, and also stipulates and agrees that no white person or persons shall be permitted to settle upon or occupy any portion of the same; or without the consent of the Indians first had and obtained."

The "unceded Indian territory" clause was vague and confusing, and it later would become controversial. Non-reservation Lakota could hunt there "so long as the buffalo may range thereon in such numbers to justify the chase." But what if the buffalo disappeared? Article 11 dictated that the Lakota were not allowed to "occupy" those lands, but then what did "unceded" territory mean? General Sherman thought he knew. He wrote, "We have now

As a member of the peace commission, General William T. Sherman was charged with setting up military outposts in the region where the transcontinental railroad was being built. He also was to expand the network of government authority. In 1868, Sherman (*facing foreword, third from left*) met with the Lakota to sign the second Treaty of Fort Laramie.

selected and provided reservations for all, off the great roads. All who cling to their old hunting grounds are hostile and will remain so until killed off."

The treaty, in anticipation of the disappearance of the buffalo, also aimed to change the Lakota from nomadic buffalo hunters to sedentary farmers. The government agreed to give clothing, seed, farm animals, and farm equipment to the Lakota. They would even establish schools with compulsory education. To what degree the Lakota understood these treaty stipulations is still debated. One stipulation they definitely understood, however, was that the treaty could not be changed without the approval of three-quarters of the adult males of the tribe.

In May 1868, the U.S. Army abandoned the three forts, and the jubilant Lakota burned them all almost before the departing soldiers had disappeared over the first ridge. The Bozeman Trail was closed and the country again belonged to the Lakota. They would hold it for less than a decade.

THE LOSSES ADD UP

One noted feature of Crazy Horse's life was his relative lack of concern for tribal norms. He never expressed any real interest in the Sun Dance rite and rarely bothered with the ordeals of Lakota purification. When the Lakota moved camp, Crazy Horse often rode alone, off to one side of the column. People thought that he was a little bit strange. Among the Lakota, he inspired awe, reverence, excitement, jealousy, and fear.

In 1868, Crazy Horse was about 28 years old. He stood about five feet eight—medium height for a Lakota man. To many, he seemed slender. He plaited his waist-length hair in two braids that hung down in a lightly colored wave. He dressed plainly and fought in just a breechcloth and moccasins. According to Short Buffalo, who knew him well, Crazy Horse was "not very tall and not very short, neither broad nor thin. His hair was very light. . . . Crazy Horse had a very light complexion, much lighter than other Indians. His face was not broad and he had a high, sharp nose. . . ."

Although Crazy Horse was eligible to attend councils, he rarely showed any interest in politics. He Dog said, "He never spoke in council and attended very few. There was no special reason for it; it was just his nature." He did not usually concern himself with large questions (such as relations with Americans) or small ones (the site of the next camp). "He had no ambition to be a chief," said one Lakota.

Crazy Horse did not allow for his picture be taken, believing that the white man's magic box would capture his soul. This painting by Robert Ottokar Lindneux is purported to be of Crazy Horse.

"He was a very quiet man except when there was fighting," summarized He Dog. He rarely joked or smiled. "All the Lakotas like to sing and dance," said Black Elk, "but he never joined a dance, and they say nobody ever heard him sing. But everybody liked him. . . . Maybe he was always part way into that world of vision." Although Crazy Horse may have been shy, he was not antisocial. He would joke in his own tipi or when on the warpath to put the warriors at ease. He was just happiest when he was harassing his enemies, stealing horses, hunting buffalo, and sharing what he had killed with the poor.

BLACK BUFFALO WOMAN

Crazy Horse was now at the age when the Lakota expected him to take a wife. Unfortunately, he fell in love with Black Buffalo Woman, one of Red Cloud's nieces and famously beautiful among the Oglala. Many people admired her, and Crazy Horse was just one of several suitors.

According to one story, sometime in the early 1860s, Crazy Horse left on a raid with several warriors. One of the men, No Water, developed a toothache and dropped out of the raiding party to return to camp. When the raid ended, Crazy Horse returned to camp to find that Black Buffalo Woman had married No Water. Some people claim that Red Cloud had engineered the match because No Water's older brother had influence on the tribal council. Crazy Horse was crushed. He supposedly stayed in his lodge for three days and then left the camp, telling no one where he was going or when he would return.

A century later, it is hard to separate out fact from gossip in Lakota private affairs. What is known for sure, however, is that Crazy Horse did not forget the matter. Even though she was married, Black Buffalo Woman remained the love of Crazy Horse's life. Black Buffalo Woman and No Water had three children, yet Crazy Horse still lingered by No Water's lodge as much as possible.

THE SHIRT WEARERS

Around 1868 (some accounts say 1865), the senior generation of Oglala Shirt Wearers prepared to step down and nominate successors. The Shirt Wearers were supposed to serve as role models of how Lakota men should behave. A Shirt Wearer's duty was to put selfish interests aside and think always of the welfare of the tribe. Oglala elders honored four young men by holding a ceremony in which they received a colorful shirt fringed with hair locks as a sign of their position. The shirts were "owned by the tribe" and could be recalled if a wearer acted improperly.

The four young men chosen to be Shirt Wearers were Young Man Afraid of His Horse, American Horse, Sword Owner, and Crazy Horse. This was a very great honor for Crazy Horse, a young man from an undistinguished family. He was chosen for his courage, for his skill in war, and for his charity. As a Shirt Wearer, he was expected to keep little for himself. This was not a problem for Crazy Horse, who still followed his vision and gave almost everything away.

With his appointment as a Shirt Wearer, Crazy Horse had reached the top of Lakota society. To many Lakota, he seemed to display the four virtues that the tribe most admired: courage, fortitude, generosity, and wisdom. The people recognized him as one of the greatest warriors in a culture that gave the highest honors to great warriors.

DISGRACE

In May 1870, Crazy Horse was still a single man and his great passion for Black Buffalo Woman had not decreased. She apparently felt strongly about him, too, but she never divorced No Water. That would mean she would lose all her property rights and claim to her children. Ideally, Lakota marriages lasted for a lifetime, but sometimes divorces did occur. A Lakota divorce did not involve a ceremony or legal proceedings. Instead, a couple jointly decided to separate, or a husband or wife might singly choose to end the marriage. According to Lakota custom, Crazy Horse could have made No Water a formal offer (such as several horses) for her, but he did not take this step.

Crazy Horse waited until No Water had gone on a hunt, and then he eloped with Black Buffalo Woman. According to custom, she had a right to go with Crazy Horse if she wanted to leave her husband. Most Lakota expected No Water to accept his wife's decision for the harmony of the tribe. He did not; he loved and valued his wife and had no intention of giving her up without a fight. When he returned from the hunt, he borrowed a pistol from a friend and set off to follow the lovers.

Crazy Horse and Black Buffalo Woman had not gone far when No Water burst into the lodge where they were staying. Versions of the incident differ. According to one account, No Water said something like, "Friend, I have come!" and aimed his gun. Crazy Horse rose to protect himself but Little Big Man, a close friend of Crazy

Horse, may have grabbed his arm as he was rising to meet the challenge. Yet some versions do not mention Little Big Man at all.

No one disputes that No Water then shot Crazy Horse just below his left nostril. The bullet made a surface wound along the line of his teeth and fractured his upper jaw before leaving his neck at the base of his skull. Fortunately for all, Crazy Horse did not die, but he would need to nurse his painful jaw for several months before regaining his strength.

The Lakota camp was in a complete uproar. Crazy Horse's people and No Water's people prepared to fight. "For a while," remembered He Dog, "it looked as if a lot of blood would flow." The Lakota peacemakers had to work quickly to prevent what could become a bloody feud. In the end, No Water gave Crazy Horse his best horse as a peace offering and Black Buffalo Woman was persuaded to return to her husband. In this situation, a reclaimed woman could expect to be physically punished or even mutilated by her husband. No Water agreed to the condition that she should not be punished, and she was not.

Not surprisingly, Crazy Horse and No Water never really made up. Black Buffalo Woman's fourth child, a daughter, had a noticeably lighter complexion. Gossips said she was the daughter of Crazy Horse, but as He Dog said, "it was never known for certain." Supposedly, Crazy Horse once met No Water on a hunt and chased him across the Yellowstone River before allowing him to escape. Neither did No Water forget. He was an eager member of the party that arrested Crazy Horse in the incident that led to his death in 1877.

No Water's attempt to murder Crazy Horse was clearly a criminal act by Lakota standards. Still, Crazy Horse was not blameless, especially given his role as a Shirt Wearer. He had taken another man's wife with little regard for the consequences. His passion had seriously threatened tribal unity. Crazy Horse could no longer be a Shirt Wearer. According to one story, Crazy Horse brought the shirt to the council tipi, saying simply, "I'd rather be a plain warrior. I'm not an orator, I'm not a politician."

It was clear to the Lakota that, for the good of the tribe, Crazy Horse needed to get married. Before the Black Buffalo Woman incident, Crazy Horse had been involved in a passionless courtship with a woman named Black Shawl. He had never seemed particularly excited about the match. Now the relationship was renewed, and Crazy Horse married Black Shawl barely a month after his disastrous elopement with Black Buffalo Woman.

Although somewhat of an arranged marriage, Crazy Horse grew to love Black Shawl. One oral tradition noted that Crazy Horse "was always by himself. He made his own power. When someone wanted him, they could always get his wife, Black Shawl, to go after him." The couple had one daughter—They Are Afraid of Her—who supposedly looked like Crazy Horse. According to some accounts, Crazy Horse was a very devoted father who doted on his daughter.

Around this time, the Lakota made him tribal war chief, replacing Red Cloud. Crazy Horse would now have decision-making power in military strategy, tactics, and negotiations. He was universally recognized as the Oglala's greatest warrior. Then things began to go wrong. In 1869 and 1870, Crazy Horse took a larger role in organizing war parties, attacking straggling miners, and harassing isolated settlements in the Powder River country. He also continued raiding the Crow and Shoshone. In one battle against the Shoshone in 1870, his older mentor, Hump, was killed. The two had argued about tactics, with Crazy Horse wanting to avoid a fight and Hump looking for one. After Hump's death, one Lakota said that Crazy Horse was so "beside himself with grief and rage . . . [that from] that very hour . . . Crazy Horse sought death."

Another tragedy occurred at about the same time. Little Hawk, his reckless little brother, was killed when he foolishly attacked some well-armed miners. Many older men of the tribe thought Little Hawk would be a greater warrior than Crazy Horse, but Little Hawk was too impulsive. Crazy Horse received the news of his death shortly after his marriage to Black Shawl. He had always been deeply attached to his younger brother. When he recovered from his face wound, Crazy Horse rode south, gathered up his brother's remains, and buried them.

More misfortune followed. Around 1873, They Are Afraid of Her died of cholera while Crazy Horse was away on a raid against the Crow. The camp had moved about 70 miles (112 km) during his absence. When he returned and found that she had died, he rode two days through Crow territory to locate her burial scaffold. Extremely upset, he mourned there with no food or water for three days.

By the early 1870s, Crazy Horse's personal losses began to pile up. Hump, Lone Bear, and Little Hawk had been killed in battle. His only child had died from cholera. His one great love affair had ended in disaster. Crazy Horse was more determined than ever to live apart from the Americans as long as the game held out, but even that was going wrong.

THE SLAUGHTER OF THE BUFFALO

At the Second Treaty of Fort Laramie, the U.S. government guaranteed the Lakota the right to hunt on certain lands "so long as the buffalo may range thereon in such numbers as to justify the chase." Yet at the same time, Americans worked to exterminate buffalo herds. Unable to defeat Native Americans in pitched battle, the U.S. Army waged war on the animals on which Lakota culture depended.

White Americans wanted the Lakota to give up the life of nomadic hunter-warriors and settle down on reservations to make new lives as farmers. In 1867, well-meaning peace commissioners said, "We say to you that the buffalo will not last for ever. They are now becoming few and you must know it. When that day, the Indian must change the road his father trod, or he must suffer, and probably die." However, the Plains tribes preferred to hunt buffalo as long as there were buffalo to hunt. "The time has not come for us yet to go a-farming," said one Lakota in 1867. "When the game is all gone, I will let [you] know that we are willing."

By the 1870s, the abundance of game on the Plains was clearly disappearing. Native Americans were not blameless in the destruction of the buffalo herds, but the Plains tribes generally had an almost religious respect toward the earth and its creatures. The white

The December 12, 1874, issue of *Harper's Magazine* reported on the slaughter of the buffalo. Hunters on the plains boasted of killing up to 2,000 in one season, and trains carried loads of amateur hunters who fired upon the animals from their car windows. This indiscriminate slaughter would cause the near extinction of the buffalo and lead to wars between American Indians and white settlers.

attitude was strictly commercial. American bison hunting was a huge industry involving thousands of people. Whites used buffalo skins for robes and rugs, crushed the bones to make china and fertilizer, and exported bison hides to Europe. A professional hunter could kill more than 100 animals at a single stand. One professional hunter claimed to have killed more than 20,000. "Ahh, my heart fell down," said one Native American woman, "when I began to see dead buffalo scattered all over our beautiful country, killed, and skinned, and left to rot by white men, many, many hundreds of buffalo. . . ."

The slaughter of the buffalo, so harmful to the Native American tribes, was also a conscious military strategy. Generals such as Sherman and Philip Sheridan had defeated the Confederacy by waging total war. They now applied the same strategy in their assaults on the Plains tribes. Killing buffalo was much easier than killing Native Americans and a more effective way of defeating them. Warriors who never would have thought to surrender looked at their starving families, came to the agencies, and accepted government rations.

The great buffalo herds were reduced from an estimated 50 million in 1800 to 15 million in 1850 to about 2,000 in 1900. "Kill every buffalo you can," advised one army officer. "Every buffalo dead is an Indian gone." In their place, whites substituted cattle on the vast grazing lands. "A cold wind blew across the prairie when the last buffalo fell," said Sitting Bull, "a death wind for my people."

U.S. NATIVE AMERICAN POLICY

During Ulysses Grant's presidency (1869–1877), approximately 300,000 Native Americans lived in the lands west of the Mississippi River, with probably about 75,000 on the Great Plains. After the Civil War, the millions of acres of fertile farmland and national resources in the West became a target for American farmers, ranchers, miners, and speculators. The white population between the Mississippi River and the Pacific Ocean increased from 7 million in 1870 to 17 million in 1890. The result was small-scale warfare between whites and Native Americans that cost millions of dollars and the lives of 25 soldiers for every Native American killed.

The Department of the Interior supervised tribal affairs, but its agents regularly cheated Native Americans. Army officers squabbled frequently with Indian agents over policy, and an "Indian Ring" in Washington, D.C. typically stole funds and supplies intended for reservation Natives. "No branch of the national government is so spotted with fraud, so tainted with corruption . . . as this Indian Bureau," charged Representative James Garfield in 1869.

Early United States treaties had described Native American tribes as independent "nations." In the 1830s, the Supreme Court declared that Native Americans were "domestic dependent nations" subject to Washington's "dominion and control." In 1871, Congress ended the treaty system, which implied two near-equal sides, and replaced it with informal agreements made by the Indian office with the tribes. In the so-called *Cherokee Tobacco* case in 1871, the Supreme Court stated that Congress could disregard previous treaties with Native American tribes. In most ways, the legal status of American Indians resembled that of slaves before the Civil War; they were neither citizens nor aliens, but simply subjects.

In his 1872 annual report, Francis Amasa Walker, the commissioner of Indian Affairs, suggested bribing Native Americans with promises of food and gifts to lure them to reservations where the United States could "civilize" them. Walker suggested that coercion would be necessary because Native Americans were "unused to manual labor and physically unqualified for it by habits of the chase ... without forethought and without self control ... with strong animal appetites and no intellectual tastes or aspirations to hold those appetites in check."

THE NORTHERN PACIFIC RAILROAD

When Red Cloud moved to the reservation, several thousand Lakota stayed behind. They had not closed the Bozeman Trail and burned the forts to live at the Red Cloud Agency and receive food in boxes and sacks. They had fought the whites to hunt the buffalo. Native Americans who refused to sign the Second Treaty of Fort Laramie included Sitting Bull, Crazy Horse, Gall, and Two Moons. The non-treaty Natives set up their lodges in the valleys of the clear rivers of the "unceded" Powder River country and tried their best to preserve their old way of life. Some of the reservation Natives would join their relatives on a seasonal basis. They would leave the agency to hunt and socialize in the summer and return to draw government rations in the winter. Almost alone, Crazy Horse declined to trade or even to visit the agencies.

The Americans, however, did not leave the non-treaty Lakota in peace. After the completion of the first transcontinental railroad in 1869, the U.S. government drew up plans for a second route to

While Red Cloud led attacks against forts in Powder River country during the Red Cloud War, Sitting Bull (*above*) led his own attacks on small forts throughout the upper Missouri area. Crazy Horse and Sitting Bull refused to sign the Fort Laramie treaties, instead choosing to fight for their land.

link the Great Lakes with the Pacific Northwest. General Sherman praised the Northern Pacific Railroad because it "would help take land from savages and turn it into cattle range, farms, and mines." Sherman told General Sheridan to give the railroad survey crews all his support because the Northern Pacific would "help to bring the Indian problem to a final solution." In 1871, railroad survey crews appeared in Lakota territory to find the best route to and across the northern Rockies.

The Lakota were determined to resist this newest treaty violation. They knew that the railroad would chase the buffalo away. One war chief said that he would "personally fight the railroad people as long as he lived, would tear up the road, and kill its builders." He would have his chance, for in the late summer of 1872, a force of several hundred soldiers pushed up the Yellowstone River into eastern Montana to escort the Northern Pacific survey crew.

Crazy Horse and Sitting Bull joined forces to resist the intrusion of the survey crews and the soldiers. At the Battle of Arrow Creek, the well-armed American soldiers held off the Lakota. In the middle of this battle, Sitting Bull astonished everyone, Lakota and soldier alike. He sat down in the middle of a meadow, in range of American riflemen, casually filled a pipe, and smoked it while bullets cut the grass all around him. Then he carefully cleaned the pipe and returned to Lakota lines. Crazy Horse, perhaps jealous, then made a reckless charge, with his horse shot out from under him. The battle was inconclusive, but it did nothing to harm the reputations of the two great Lakota leaders.

The next summer, the inconclusive Battle of the Yellowstone (sometimes called the Battle of Honsinger Bluff) was probably the first meeting between Crazy Horse and George Custer. Custer was leading a large army force that was marching through Lakota country. Near the meeting of the Tongue and Yellowstone rivers, Sitting Bull and Crazy Horse tried to check their advance. They attempted the decoy technique, but it did not work. Some Lakota and Cheyenne charged, but Custer's men drove them off and the Natives disengaged. Custer admitted that the Native charge was "in perfect line, and with as seeming good order and alignment as the best drilled cavalry." However, he drew the wrong conclusion from the skirmish. In accounts he wrote later, Custer did not take the Lakota's fighting abilities too seriously, mistaking a planned withdrawal for cowardice.

Sitting Bull (1831–1890)

Crazy Horse probably first worked with Sioux chief Sitting Bull in about 1871. The two men had very different personalities, but on the major issue of the day—the Lakota relationship to the Americans—they saw eye-to-eye. Both were uncompromising opponents of American expansion.

Sitting Bull's fame among his own people rested on his spirituality as much as his military skill. He was about eight years older than Crazy Horse, and his generosity was as famous among the Hunkpapa as Crazy Horse's among the Oglala. Unlike his Oglala counterpart, however, Sitting Bull was a clever politician, a spellbinding orator, and a wily negotiator.

One Cheyenne chief noted that Sitting Bull was "the most consistent advocate of the idea of living out of all touch with white people." He wanted no part of treaties, agents, or rations. Crazy Horse and Sitting Bull would have preferred to avoid whites altogether. They wanted nothing more than to follow the buffalo and raid enemy tribes as their parents and grandparents had done. This option, however, was not open to them. The whites were too many and wanted too much.

Throughout the 1870s, Sitting Bull and Crazy Horse worked together to prevent American expansion into Lakota territory. The two helped mastermind the defeat of Custer's cavalry at the Battle of the Little Bighorn. After that, Sitting Bull and some of his followers fled to Canada, but they returned in 1881 and were placed on a reservation. In 1885, he appeared for four months in Buffalo Bill's Wild West show. In the last years, he encouraged the Lakota to hold onto their lands, and he supported the Ghost Dance. Native American police tried to arrest Sitting Bull in 1890 on a charge of anti-white activities. Like Crazy Horse, he was killed while "resisting arrest."

The Northern Pacific Railroad was not stopped by the Lakota but by events on Wall Street when the financial panic of 1873 led to a depression in the United States. The Northern Pacific went bankrupt, and construction of the railroad stalled at Bismarck, North Dakota, for six years. Nevertheless, a new problem arose to threaten the Lakota homeland.

THE REVOLT
OF THE LAKOTA

In 1873, prospectors began to explore the Black Hills inside the Great Sioux Reservation. The whites were looking for gold, an especially valuable rock in the midst of a national depression. The presence of these miners completely violated the well-publicized second Treaty of Fort Laramie, which had unusually clear provisions that the Black Hills belonged to the Lakota and that whites must stay out. The whites, however, did not care. If gold were discovered on Lakota land, then the land would just have to be taken from them and given to white Americans. As Red Cloud would later say of Americans, "They made us many promises, more than I can remember, but they never kept but one. They promised to take our land and they took it."

To the Lakota, the Black Hills were a sacred place where spirits lived. They called the Black Hills *Paha Sapa*, the center of the world. Young warriors sometimes went there on vision quests. Now gold seekers were digging up the heart of their world.

In 1874, Custer led a group of soldiers to help survey the Black Hills for a military post and to look for gold. The expedition was out and back in less than two months, almost before the Lakota knew what was happening. The expedition helped to popularize the notion that gold was easy to find in the Black Hills. The trail that Custer blazed became known to the Lakota as the "Thieves' Road."

By the winter of 1875–1876, as many as 15,000 white miners camped illegally in Lakota territory. There were as many miners as there were people in the entire Lakota nation. The U.S. government refused to enforce the Fort Laramie Treaty. Instead, the Grant administration tried to pressure the Lakota to sell the sacred Black Hills.

Even after a century of dealing with whites, the Lakota had difficulty understanding the American obsession with gold and private land ownership. The Lakota regarded the earth as their "mother" because it helped them survive. They did not really believe that land could be owned in the same way that a person could own a pony or a blanket. The Lakota thought that people could not buy land because it was part of nature; it was like buying the sun or the sky.

In 1870, Red Cloud went to Washington, D.C., and told the government, "I have two mountains in that country—the Black Hills and the Big Horn Mountain. I want the Father to make no roads through them. I have told these things three times; now I have come here to tell them the fourth time." However, in 1874, Red Cloud was an agency chief. Based on history, he assumed that the Americans were going to take the Black Hills no matter what the Lakota did. For this reason, he believed the Lakota should bargain for the best price rather than see the land taken for nothing (which is eventually what happened).

Red Cloud's position, however, was unpopular with the Lakota people. "We called Red Cloud's people 'Hangs-Around-The-Fort,'" said Black Elk, "and our people said they were standing up for the wasichus [whites], and if we did not do something we should lose the Black Hills." Yet even Red Cloud would not take responsibility for selling sacred land. The agency chiefs declined to change their minds, even when threatened with the loss of food rations at their agencies and the refusal of the government to keep miners out of the region.

The U.S. government decided on a showdown. If the Lakota would not sell the Black Hills, then the United States would take the Powder River country, which was not officially part of the

Lakota reservation. In November 1875, the commissioner of Indian Affairs announced that any Natives who lived in the Powder River country threatened the reservation system. The U.S. government ordered Sitting Bull, Crazy Horse, and the other "hostiles" to leave their hunting grounds in the "unceded lands" at once and report to the Great Sioux Reservation by February 1.

Nothing in the Forty Laramie Treaty gave the government any right to restrict the Native American use of the Powder River country. Nevertheless, Crazy Horse did not appeal to the treaty, which he had never signed anyway. Instead, he sent back word that the winter was an inconvenient time to move. In the spring of 1876, the U.S. Army sent soldiers to round up the "hostile" Lakota and bring them in by force.

THE REYNOLDS FIGHT

The winter of 1875–1876 would be Crazy Horse's last winter as a free Lakota warrior. Herds of buffalo still roamed the Powder River country. The hostiles were well armed and determined. The Lakota had suffered some setbacks but they had avoided crushing defeats. They believed that the spiritual powers of the universe would continue to assist them in their just cause. Although in retrospect the Lakota cause seems hopeless, the non-treaty Lakota did not see it that way at the time.

Whites living in the West constantly promoted the idea that hordes of bloodthirsty Native Americans were threatening America. Yet in 1876, probably no more than 3,500 Lakota and Cheyenne belonged to the free-living bands that rarely visited an agency. Of this number, about 1,000 were warriors. Most major Lakota leaders had accepted that the old way of life was rapidly ending. One way or another, they would have to walk the white man's road or else fight until all the Lakota were killed. It was a particularly stark choice, with Red Cloud and Spotted Tail on one side and Crazy Horse and Sitting Bull on the other. There was not a lot of room in the middle.

In the spring of 1876, General Sheridan made plans to smash the "hostiles" who, although they had done nothing over the

General George Crook was considered the U.S. Army's greatest Indian fighter. He achieved great success in influencing American Indians onto reservations because of his extensive use of Indian scouts and his readiness to negotiate rather than force conflict.

winter, were now considered to be at war against the U.S. government. Sheridan ordered three columns of about 2,500 men, led by Alfred Terry, John Gibbon, and George Crook, to converge on the Yellowstone River area. Sheridan expected the army to find the Lakota, surround them, and accept their surrender or annihilate them.

The force was probably the largest ever sent out to do battle with Native Americans on the Plains.

George Crook (1828–1890) was the greatest "Indian fighter" ever produced by the U.S. Army. After attending the U.S. Military Academy at West Point, Crook spent the 1850s battling Native tribes in northern California and southern Oregon. During the Civil War, Crook performed well, sometimes brilliantly, and always courageously under fire. On the Great Plains, Crook was an unusual general in many ways. He often chose to ride a mule rather than a horse, and he rarely wore his uniform in the field. Crook did not drink alcohol, coffee, or tea; his great passion was hunting, which he pursued at every opportunity. He knew how to pack a mule, mend a saddle, throw a lariat, and cook a meal in the field. As a commander, he was easy to respect, but hard to like.

Crook was a mass of contradictions. He believed that the U.S. government and army caused almost all Indian problems. "All the tribes tell the same story," he wrote. "They are surrounded on all sides, the game is destroyed or driven away; they are left to starve, and there remains but one thing for them to do—fight while they can." At the same time, Crook believed Native Americans were doomed to extinction or assimilation. He worked all his life to destroy their cultures, hunt down their warriors, and seize their land.

Crook's men left Fort Fetterman on March 1 and headed north on a scouting trip. Two weeks later, Colonel J. Reynolds came across a Native American village. His scouts assured him that the village belonged to Crazy Horse, but in fact it was a Cheyenne village under He Dog and Two Moons. Reynolds's men made a dawn attack, captured the village, and destroyed a great deal of supplies, but they killed few warriors. Some Cheyenne counterattacked, and Reynolds ordered a hasty withdrawal. Crook was furious, not because Reynolds did not know whom he was attacking, but that Crook had needlessly destroyed supplies he could have used. Crook retreated to Fort Fetterman and had Reynolds court-martialed. To the end of his life, neither man ever admitted that they had made a mistake and had attacked a nonhostile village.

The incident, sometimes known as the Powder River Fight or the Reynolds Fight, enraged the Lakota and Cheyenne. Although they were aware of the order to report to the Great Sioux Reservation, they did not think they were at war with the United States and did not think the army would attack them. The Reynolds Fight only solidified the Cheyenne-Lakota alliance, aroused the bands, and brought talk of revenge. Crazy Horse said that "he would now strike a blow that would be remembered by those who invaded his country." It was not a good start to the great white offensive.

SOLDIERS FALLING INTO CAMP

Meanwhile, thousands of Native American warriors were gathering to fight the soldiers. Sitting Bull had sent runners to every Lakota and Cheyenne band for hundreds of miles around, on the reservation and off, summoning them to a great war council on Rosebud Creek in southern Montana. "We must stand together or they will rub us out separately," Sitting Bull said. "They want war. All right, we'll give it to them."

By June 1876, an enormous camp had formed on the Rosebud. Hundreds of newcomers arrived each week. As many as 15,000 Native Americans had gathered, including about 2,500 warriors. It was one of the largest Native American armies ever assembled on the continent. Lakota and Cheyenne tipis stretched for several miles along the banks of the Rosebud. The number was swollen by people from the Lakota agencies who had left the reservation to join their non-agency kin for summer hunting and ritual ceremonial activities. "We supposed that the combined camps would frighten off the soldiers," recalled Wooden Leg. "Then we could separate again into the tribal bands and resume our quiet wandering and hunting."

The Lakota were extremely confident. In June, as they prepared for war, they held a Sun Dance. Sitting Bull, the Hunkpapa war chief, was also a spiritual leader and holy man. He decided to seek divine guidance by participating in the ancient religious ritual of self-torture. Sitting Bull had 50 pieces of flesh cut from his arms and chest and underwent other tests of courage. The result was the best-reported vision in Native American history. Sitting Bull "dreamed" he saw hundreds of upside-down U.S. Army soldiers falling like grasshoppers into the Native American camp. It was a clear omen that the Lakota would be victorious. Sitting Bull's vision made the Lakota and Cheyenne warriors eager to fight.

THE BATTLE OF THE ROSEBUD

General Crook led the strongest of the three pincers that were supposed to crush the last resistance of the Lakota. On June 16, 1876, Lakota scouts spotted Crooks's advance column. The next day, warriors led by Crazy Horse surprised Crook as he camped beside Rosebud Creek. The two sides were evenly matched; Crook had about 1,200 men, while Crazy Horse led a force of between 750 and 1,500.

The Battle of the Rosebud was a mad, swirling fight. The Lakota and Cheyenne kept up constant pressure on the U.S. soldiers, riding among them and sometimes splitting them into small groups. There was a great deal of charging and counter-charging, noise, dust, and the smell of burning gunpowder. Both sides fought bravely in one of North America's only pitched battles on open ground between relatively equal forces of soldiers and Native Americans. "Until the sun went far toward the west there were charges back and forth," Wooden Leg recalled. "Our Indians fought and ran away, fought and ran away. The soldiers and their Indian scouts did the same. Sometimes we chased them, sometimes they chased us."

Crook tried desperately to form a defensive line. He was helped, if not saved, by his Crow and Shoshone scouts, who threw back several Lakota attacks that threatened to overwhelm the American soldiers. Meanwhile, Crazy Horse, Black Twin, and the Lakota were just as determined. Crook struggled all day to launch a counteroffensive, but the Natives prevented him.

Crazy Horse was in the forefront of the fighting in the Battle of the Rosebud. He encouraged his warriors to greater feats with his famous war cry, "Come on Lakotas, it's a good day to die. Cowards to the rear!" One Lakota distinctly remembered Crazy Horse amazingly surviving a hail of bullets, recalling that "they couldn't

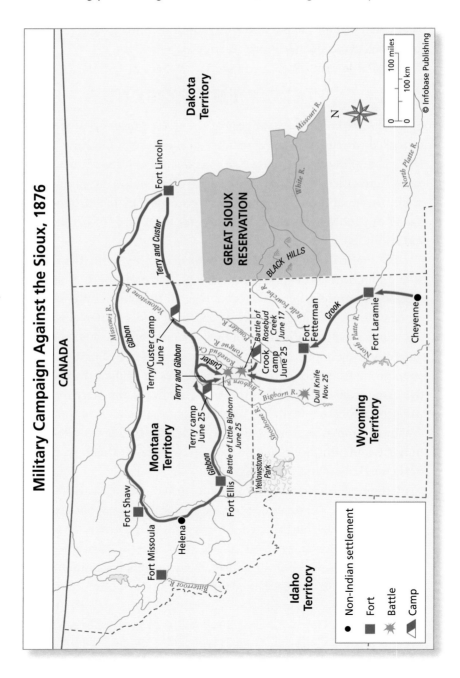

even hit his horse." At one point, when the Lakota began to fall back, Crazy Horse and several other chiefs rode among them and inspired them to return to battle. The Lakota still fought in independent swarms, but the influence of the war chief's bravery allowed Crazy Horse to exert some loose tactical control over the Lakota warriors.

The Battle of the Rosebud lasted an amazing six hours. The Lakota and Cheyenne fought in an unusually disciplined manner, fighting for a victory more than for counting coup. Early in the afternoon, however, they started to break off the fighting and drift away. They had not been defeated but, as one of the warriors later explained, "They were tired and hungry so they went home." As in many battles on the Plains, a great deal of shooting led to very few casualties. Crook's 1,000 men fired more than 25,000 rounds of ammunition. The exact casualty counts are unclear, but both sides suffered about 20 dead.

That night, Crook camped in the same place as the night before, not far from where the battle began. Crook's official report claimed victory: "My troops beat these Indians on a field of their own choosing and drove them in utter rout from it. . . ." Actually, Crook himself considered the Battle of the Rosebud a defeat. It was his only one in his decades of warfare with Native Americans, and he was sensitive about it for the rest of his life. The army had fought well, but Crazy Horse had protected the distant village and also halted Crook's advance.

As one of Crook's officers wrote, "we had been most humiliatingly defeated." Crook ordered his soldiers to fall back to his base of supply on Goose Creek, 40 miles away. This delayed his rendezvous with Colonel John Gibbon and General Alfred Terry. Crazy Horse had helped ruin the army's strategy of launching a three-pronged attack on the people living on the Little Bighorn River.

(*opposite*) In response to an effort by the U.S. government to break the Fort Laramie Treaty of 1868 and remove the Sioux to a smaller reservation, the Sioux conducted a marauding campaign to push white settlers out of the Black Hills altogether. George Crook's forces were defeated by Crazy Horse on June 17, eight days before George Custer's men were killed at Little Bighorn.

Native American Scouts

General Crook strongly supported the use of Native American scouts. He believed that American soldiers were no match for Native guerrilla warriors. Large forces of soldiers, dragging mostly useless equipment, could rarely catch hostile Natives. In 1866, Congress established the Indian Scouting Service as a permanent branch of the army. From that date, the army enlisted Native American scouts on the Army payroll. The program was a success; from 1872 to 1890, 16 Native American scouts received the Congressional Medal of Honor.

Recruitment for the Native scouts was not difficult because great hatreds existed between various tribes. Although the tribes on the Plains shared a similar culture, they had separate homelands and did not always like each other. They usually lacked any central leadership and did not see their common interest. These divisions played into the U.S. Army's hands.

The Crow, in particular, felt that the Lakota had stolen their lands. "The Lakota have trampled upon our hearts," said one Crow chief in 1876. "We shall spit upon their scalps." The Crow saw alliance with the United States as the last and best hope of preserving their homeland from their old enemies. The Arikara also despised the Lakota for the Lakota's constant raiding. For Native Americans now on the reservation, scouting for the army was one of the only ways to follow the traditional life of a warrior.

GEORGE ARMSTRONG CUSTER (1839–1876)

George Armstrong Custer was known as the "Boy General." At age 23, he was the youngest man to rise to the rank of general in American history. Custer came to the Plains with a brilliant reputation as a flamboyant and impulsive soldier. He was a man of astounding courage and boundless energy who never seemed to feel any fear. In the Civil War, he had 11 horses shot out from under him.

Native American scouts claimed to be realists who understood the U.S. Army's overwhelming advantage in numbers and weapons. "I . . . well remember that when white men found gold in the Black Hills the Lakota and Cheyenne made war on them," remembered Crow chief Plenty Coups.

We knew the white men were strong, without number in their own country, and that there was no good in fighting them; so that when other tribes wished us to fight them we refused. . . . Our decision was reached, not because we loved the white man . . . or because we hated the Lakota, Cheyenne, and Arapaho, but because we plainly saw that this course was the only one which might save our beautiful country for us.

To some extent, the Crow alliance with the Americans worked. Today, despite losing millions of acres to white greed, the Crow Indian Reservation is the largest reservation in Montana. The 2.2 million acres of rolling upland plains stand in the heart of the territory Crow warriors battled to defend in the 1800s.

In 1876, Crook even enrolled about 50 Lakota to fight against their relatives. The Lakota scouts knew that Crazy Horse and Sitting Bull might win some battles, but they believed continued warfare would only lead to useless suffering and would further hurt Lakota claims to their hunting grounds.

Custer's soldiers became famous for their daring charges and long, fast marches. He was an extremely aggressive commander; his 3rd Michigan suffered the highest casualties of any federal cavalry unit during the Civil War.

Custer's career in the West had not been as successful. Mostly through his own bad decisions and actions, Custer had lost much of his popularity. The army had court-martialed Custer in 1867, found him guilty of 5 of 11 charges, and suspended him from rank and command for one year. In 1876, another incident left him in disgrace with President Grant and General Sheridan. He had to beg them to get permission to lead his 7th Cavalry (under Alfred Terry) on the campaign against the Lakota.

Pictured is George Custer (*seated*) with his Indian scouts in 1873. His announcement of finding gold in the Black Hills triggered the gold rush in Sioux territory.

In fact, Custer was victorious in only one engagement against Native Americans. In November 1868, in the so-called Battle of Washita in Oklahoma, Custer marched his men through heavy snow to attack a village of peaceful Cheyenne under Black Kettle. The Natives did not consider themselves at war and were taken by surprise. Custer's men slaughtered at least 50 men, women, and children—less than half of the dead Cheyenne were warriors. For this, eastern newspapers called the dashing Custer a great "Indian fighter."

Custer's orders were to probe west along the Rosebud and into the valley of the Little Bighorn to look for Natives. Terry and Gibbon would ascend the Yellowstone River and lower Bighorn River and crush the Native tribes between them. It was supposed to be a coordinated campaign, and Custer had been specifically warned not to attack until reinforcements arrived. Custer's commanders, however, knew his reputation, and the orders arguably left him some leeway to act alone if the situation arose.

Custer had very experienced Native American scouts, such as Mitch Boyer, Bloody Knife, and Half Yellow Face. They all told Custer they would die if they descended into the valley where the Lakota and Cheyenne were camped. In all of their years on the Plains, none had ever seen a Native American encampment so large. Custer decided to ignore them.

According to legend, the scout Half Yellow Face then told Custer that they would all go home that day by a road they did not know. Another story relates how Bloody Knife, Custer's favorite scout, stared at the sun for a long time that morning, knowing that he would not be alive to see it go down behind the hills that evening.

Custer, however, could not wait to do battle with the Natives. He had always attacked and it had always worked out—"Custer's luck," military men called it. He decided to stretch his orders and send his men into battle without waiting for the reinforcements from the other army units that were on their way to join him.

7

THE LAST CAMPAIGN

In June 1876, General Custer and about 600 troops headed for the Little Bighorn River in southeastern Montana. Custer's Crow and Arikara scouts warned him that there was a large Native village in the area, bigger than they had ever seen. Custer brushed these warnings aside. He refused the offer of extras troops and a Gatling gun (a primitive machine gun) for fear that it might slow him down and allow the "hostiles" to get away.

Instead, Custer put together his own plan. He decided to attack at once, even though this meant he would be going into action a day earlier than General Terry had planned. In fact, Custer had decided before the campaign began that at the first opportunity he would cut loose from Terry and Gibbon and win a great battle with his own regiment. He was as convinced as Fetterman that he could whip whatever group of Natives he could persuade to stand and face him. He did not want to have to share the glory he knew he was going to win.

Custer divided his command even though he knew he was facing a large hostile force. Captain Frederick Benteen led about 125 men to scout the hills overlooking the Native village. Major Marcus Reno and about 140 men would attack the southern end of the village. Custer and about 210 men of the 7th Cavalry swung north to attack the village from the opposite end. The pack train, with another 130 men and most of the ammunition needed for a heavy engagement, was several miles behind the rest of the force.

Custer did not make any real plan to coordinate these four groups. When he ordered Reno to attack, Benteen was 10 miles (16 km) away to the southwest. Custer did not communicate any instructions to the commanders of the several units except one vague order to Reno to "charge afterward, and you will be supported by the whole outfit." On the afternoon of June 25, Reno's men attacked the Lakota-Cheyenne camp and caught them by surprise. Then, things went wrong for the soldiers. The Lakota quickly rallied from their initial surprise, and Reno never had a chance. His 115 men, lacking any support, faced more than 1,000 shouting warriors. One Cheyenne commented, "Many hundreds of Indians were dashing to and fro in front of a body of soldiers. The soldiers were on the level valley ground and were shooting with rifles. Not many bullets were being sent back at them, but thousands of arrows were falling around them." Reno might have continued to charge the village and hoped to benefit from the chaos. Had he chosen to do so, however, he might have been totally wiped out in the attempt.

Instead, Reno tried a number of defensive positions. None would hold. Finally, his men made a panicky retreat back across the Little Bighorn and up a bluff. By 4:00 P.M., Reno had established a solid defensive position in the hills on the east bank, but half of his forces were dead, wounded, or left behind in the woods. The men were confused, dispirited, and almost out of ammunition.

Fortunately for Reno, Benteen had given up on looking for Natives in the jumble of hills, ravines, gullies, and bluffs that Custer had ordered him to search. Benteen decided, on his own authority, to go back to the regiment. On returning, he found Reno's men in desperate straits but could do little more than dig in alongside the beleaguered troops. The men were pinned there the rest of the day and into the next one (June 26), but they managed to fight off all Native American attacks. In two days of fighting, Reno and Benteen suffered about 50 killed and 50 wounded.

THE BATTLE OF
THE LITTLE BIGHORN

After sending Reno to attack the lower end of the huge camp, Custer followed him for a short distance, intending to support him as he had promised. Then he turned away to the north along the bluffs. Custer knew that Reno was fighting for his life, but he was more worried that the Natives in the enormous village across the river would get away. Custer had convinced himself that the 7th Cavalry was invincible under his leadership. The thousands of Natives did not represent danger to him but only another step on the ladder to fame. Custer decided to attack the other end of the village.

Perhaps Custer was trying to relieve pressure on Reno by attacking the downstream end of the village; however, Custer barely began his advance when he received word that Reno had retreated across the river. Custer had a clear choice: to press on with the attack or to retreat to a more defensive position. Custer decided to press on with the attack. He fully expected the Lakota and Cheyenne to flee.

At this point, a fog of confusion falls over the events. For more than a century, people have argued over Custer's strategy and what he was intending to do. One thing is for sure; whatever he was planning, it did not work.

Custer's five companies had been on the march for 25 of the previous 30 hours and were extremely tired. His line of battle disintegrated as Lakota and Cheyenne warriors came in a solid mass after fording the river at the lower edge of their camp. The soldiers probably faced at least 2,000 warriors. In the vanguard was Gall, the Hunkpapa chief, who had just finished throwing back Reno's attack. The battlefield soon turned into a swirling nightmare of dust, smoke, yells, curses, terror, and death. The Native Americans swept through the southern end of Custer's line and simply annihilated the two companies there.

The Lakota warriors were extremely confident that day based on Sitting Bull's vision and their recent battle with Crook at the Rosebud. "By now a big cry was going up all around the soldiers up there and the warriors were coming from everywhere and it was getting dark with dust and smoke," said one Lakota warrior. "The soldiers were all rubbed out there and scattered around."

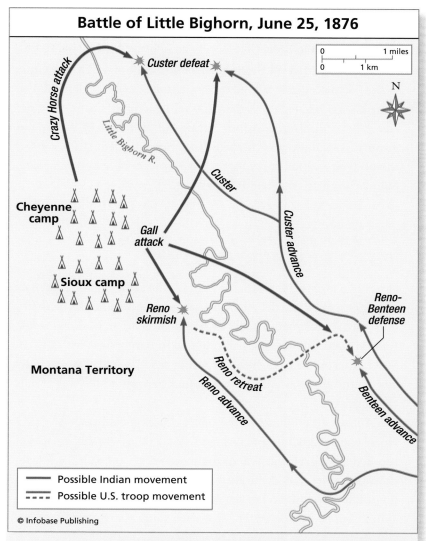

Battle of Little Bighorn, June 25, 1876

Crazy Horse attack

Little Bighorn R.

Custer defeat

Custer

Cheyenne camp

Gall attack

Sioux camp

Reno skirmish

Montana Territory

Reno retreat

Reno advance

Custer advance

Reno-Benteen defense

Benteen advance

0 ——— 1 miles
0 ——— 1 km

N

—— Possible Indian movement
- - - Possible U.S. troop movement

© Infobase Publishing

In one of the best-known battles of the Sioux Wars, Lt. Col. George Armstrong Custer's entire cavalry troop was killed when they attacked a force of mainly Cheyenne and Sioux at the Little Bighorn River on June 25, 1876. This map shows possible troop and American Indian movements in the battle.

The Lakota harried Custer so hard that the 7th Cavalry could never really establish any solid defensive position. "Custer's men in the beginning shot straight," said Iron Hawk, but "later they shot like drunken men . . . wildly in every way." Paints Himself Brown, a young warrior at the fight, said, "Pretty soon the soldiers started to run and we went after them, but it wasn't long before they were all killed and wounded."

The Battle of the Little Bighorn, or the Battle of the Greasy Grass as the Lakota called it, was all over by about 5:30 P.M. In less than an hour, Custer had led more than 260 soldiers into the worst American military disaster in history. Sitting Bull concluded, "We did not go out of our country to kill them. They came to kill us and got killed themselves. . . . I felt sorry that too many were killed on each side, but when Indians must fight, they must."

CRAZY HORSE AT THE LITTLE BIGHORN

Crazy Horse's precise role at the Battle of the Little Bighorn is a matter of guesswork and debate. Some say he rode out and skirmished a little with Reno's men. Others believe he was still in his lodge when Reno arrived and was only interested in the larger fight with Custer. Several accounts have him preparing for the battle very coolly and methodically, making sure he had performed his war rituals correctly.

Almost all accounts of the battle describe his bravery. "Crazy Horse was ahead of all, and he killed a lot of them with his war-club," recalled Flying Hawk. An Arapaho warrior said, "Crazy Horse, the Sioux chief, was the bravest man I ever saw. He rode closest to the soldiers, yelling to his warriors. All the soldiers were shooting at him, but he was never hit." However, some Native American accounts do not even mention Crazy Horse.

Many historians have written about the brilliance of Crazy Horse in flanking Custer and seizing the high ground (today called Custer Hill). According to this story, Custer turned north and

Crazy Horse played a major role in the victory against Custer and his men. Crazy Horse's command of a surprise attack on General Crook's forces later ensured Custer's defeat at the Battle of Little Bighorn. The victory was the last for American Indians in the West.

desperately attempted to establish a defensive position on the hill now named after him. Crazy Horse, leading perhaps a thousand warriors, forded the river, flanked him, and sealed Custer's doom. There is real doubt (and of course, debate), however, as to whether this charge ever occurred as described. All accounts of the battle depend on Native American memory and a study of the battleground

A Low-Status Profession

Many nineteenth-century Americans viewed a military career as a last re-sort for men who could not do anything else or were too lazy to work. The Civil War had glorified the role of the heroic soldier, but as soon as the war ended the U.S. government dismantled the military. At the end of the Civil War, the Union Army numbered 200,000 men. In 1866, Congress reduced the regular army to 56,000 men, most stationed in the South to enforce Reconstruction. The army was reduced to 45,000 men in 1869, to 30,000 men in 1870, and to 25,000 men in 1874. (In 2009, the U.S. military to-taled close to 3 million people.)

All of the men in this Native-fighting army were volunteers who had enlisted for a five-year term. The average age of the soldiers was 23. Many were recent immigrants from England, Ireland, or Germany, and most were poor. Some were attracted by the steady employment, regular rations, and free medical care offered by the army. Other recruits were rootless vet-erans of the Civil War who had lost everything or former slaves who had nothing to begin with.

itself. There is enough conflicting information to allow for many different possibilities.

Whites preferred to believe that a "red" Caesar or Napoleon led the Lakota-Cheyenne force. It did not seem as bad to whites if a military genius had annihilated the 7th Cavalry. After the Battle of the Little Bighorn, Sitting Bull and Crazy Horse filled this role. They became infamous in American society as the men whose strategy had defeated Custer. This judgment was particularly ironic in the case of Sitting Bull, who had acted as a peace chief at the battle with primary responsibility for the protection of the helpless in the village.

It is important to remember, however, that no one person had total authority in Plains Indian society, even in war. Philo Clark, who served with Crook, noted, "Great prominence has been given

Soldiering was especially difficult in the dreary frontier outposts of the northern Plains. In an 1891 report, the secretary of war reported that losses through desertion from 1867 to 1891 averaged one-third of all enlistees. Many of the soldiers of Custer's cavalry were "snowbirds," enlisting only for the winter months. When better weather came, they took better jobs on the railroad or in the mines.

The basic army unit was the "company." After 1876, each company was supposed to have 100 privates, but most were under-strength. A soldier had little contact with men outside his company. He was completely at the mercy of his noncommissioned officers, usually men of long service. He could not even speak to an officer without the permission of the first sergeant.

A wide gulf separated enlisted men from their commissioned officers. Most officers came from the upper class of society and had graduated from West Point. Many officers, assigned to a post in what they considered "the end of the world," found no friends and the duty dull. Alcoholism was a constant problem, contributing to the public impression that soldiering was a low-status profession.

to Crazy Horse and Sitting Bull in this war, the good fighting strategy, and subsequent muster by retreats being attributed to them, whereas they are really not entitled to more credit or censure than many others so far as plans and orders were concerned." Yet having written that, Clark then proceeded to give Crazy Horse a prominent role at the Little Bighorn, writing of his daring, his bravery, and the great prestige he won that day. It seems certain that Crazy Horse's role at the battle will continue to be debated for the near future.

FALLOUT FROM CUSTER'S DEFEAT

The Lakota and Cheyenne had made two mistakes at Little Bighorn. They had won too great a victory and they had won at the worst possible moment. The news of Custer's defeat reached the East in the middle of the centennial celebration of the United States' independence. White Americans were shocked and angered that a bunch of "savages" should humiliate a people who supposedly represented human progress. Western settlers called for the extermination of all Native Americans, and the U.S. government felt compelled to send an enormous and well-supplied force to defeat the Plains Indians once and for all.

The first problem for the Americans to solve was the status of the Black Hills. Within weeks of the battle, the government ordered Indian agents to withhold rations until the Lakota sold the Black Hills. An illegal council and treaty followed, and the United States stole not only the beautiful and gold-rich Black Hills but also the Powder River country, the Yellowstone River area, and the Bighorn Mountains. The agreement clearly violated the clause in the Second Fort Laramie Treaty that stated that the treaty could only be changed by a vote of three-quarters of the adult males of the tribe.

A century later, the United States admitted the illegality of the land sale. In 1974, Congress awarded the Lakota $17.5 million as compensation for the land and $85 million in interest payments. As of 2010, however, the Lakota have refused to accept any of this money. Instead, they want the Black Hills returned to them. The money is currently in a government account, collecting interest.

Custer's reputation seemed destined to the same fate as Fetterman's. Custer's defeat was far from a massacre; it was a battle in which American soldiers were poorly led, outnumbered, and crushed. It would seem that Custer was to blame; he had made the tactical decisions that resulted in his own death and the death of every man in all five of his companies. President Grant, an aggressive army officer himself, bluntly blamed the commander and told the public that the defeat "was a sacrifice of troops brought on by Custer himself, that was wholly unnecessary—wholly unnecessary." Terry and his staff accused Custer of being a foolish glory hound who disobeyed orders, skipped or disregarded all scouting, and charged almost blindly into a situation where he was quickly annihilated.

That this initial evaluation was not the final judgment was almost entirely due to Elizabeth Custer, the general's wife who outlived him by an astonishing 57 years. Elizabeth Custer became an outspoken advocate for her husband's reputation and endlessly campaigned on his behalf. She helped create the portrayal of George Custer as a gallant fallen hero, a heroic genius, and a martyr betrayed by the cowardly actions of Reno and Benteen. The glory of "Custer's Last Stand" became an iconic myth of American history for more than a century after his death.

The Battle of the Little Bighorn, devastating as it was, only temporarily delayed the march of white soldiers, settlers, and prospectors into Native American lands. In the following weeks, the U.S. government sent massive reinforcements into Lakota territory to hunt down the starving Lakota and Cheyenne bands still struggling to survive. The white conquest of the Northern Plains would come not through any decisive victory but through attrition. The Native American economy could not support resistance to the technologically and numerically superior white forces.

THE BATTLE OF SLIM BUTTES

The day after the battle, Sitting Bull and the other chiefs decided to retreat. They broke camp and split into separate bands, each taking a different direction as they vanished into the mountains. The large body of Native Americans who defeated Custer fragmented into smaller and smaller groups in the weeks after their victory, searching for game before the bitter Plains winter. The Lakota had won the battle, but the war was another story.

Crazy Horse may have spent the summer attacking the miners in the Black Hills. He worked silently and without remorse; this was Lakota land and the miners were invaders. Meanwhile, the inevitable American retaliation had begun. On September 9, 1876, General Crook's men found, attacked, and captured a Lakota village at Slim Buttes in South Dakota, just north of the Black Hills. "They fought hard there in the rain," said Black Elk, and the soldiers "chased the women and children out of their homes and took all the papa (dried bison meat) that they had made to feed themselves that winter."

The Lakota defenders sent an urgent appeal for help to Crazy Horse, who was camped about 10 miles away. Crazy Horse and about 700 warriors quickly rode northward toward the village, which was set in a depression among several hills. Crook's reinforcements, however, reached the attacking army force just as the Lakota arrived.

When the Lakota arrived at an overlook, they saw Crook's large force of well-armed soldiers surrounding the village. The Lakota fired from on top of the bluffs, but Crook formed a defensive perimeter and then set the village on fire. Crook sent forward a strong line of soldiers who eventually drove most of the warriors from their hilltop positions. Casualties on both sides were light, but Crazy Horse was not pleased with the outcome. American soldiers now roamed in the heartland of Lakota territory. The tribes were on the defensive, and the winter was coming on. The Lakota sometimes called the battle "The Fight Where We Lost the Black Hills."

FAILURE OF THE PEACE DELEGATION

General Sheridan now ordered the Powder River Expedition to carry the fight to the "hostiles" in the winter. In November, Crook and 1,100 troops surprised and defeated the Cheyenne under Dull Knife and Little Wolf. The soldiers killed many people and destroyed the Cheyenne winter camp on the Powder River in the Wyoming Territory. The Dull Knife Fight (also known as the Battle of Bates Creek) virtually ended all Cheyenne resistance. The survivors wandered around in the subzero weather without sufficient clothing, and many soon froze to death. Most surrendered, but some headed north toward the camp of Crazy Horse.

For 11 days, the freezing survivors fled over the mountains and plains. The Cheyenne cut horses open and held babies inside the steaming stomachs to give them warmth and preserve their lives. When the survivors finally reached Crazy Horse, he took them in and provided for them the best he could even though he had few supplies of his own.

General Nelson Miles was now assigned to hunt down the Lakota bands that still held out. His fur-clad troopers attacked Native American camps even when the temperature fell far below zero. He

Nelson Miles was one of the most successful Indian hunters during the Indian Wars. He made a name for himself by crushing resistance by Sioux, Nez Perce, Cheyenne, Kiowa, Comanche, Arapaho, and Bannock and was a key player in defeating Sioux chiefs Sitting Bull and Crazy Horse, Nez Perce chief Joseph, and Apache chief Geronimo.

convinced several of the important Lakota chiefs, with thousands of their followers, to surrender and come in to the reservation.

Miles badly wanted the glory of Crazy Horse's surrender. He sent out many runners promising fair treatment for Crazy Horse and his people. Near the end of the year, Crazy Horse grudgingly decided he ought to consider this option. The appearance of Dull Knife's needy Cheyenne shook Crazy Horse's determination to continue the war.

For the first time in his life, Crazy Horse agreed that his people should make an effort to negotiate peace with the United States. Under flags of truce, a delegation of five Lakota approached Miles's camp. Unfortunately, a group of Miles's Crow scouts pulled the peace delegates from their saddles and killed them. Miles admitted in his report that "the act was an unprovoked cowardly murder." He tried to make amends, but Crazy Horse fled.

Yet it was one thing for Crazy Horse to refuse to make peace but quite another to continue the war. It was a terrible winter, with subzero temperatures day after day. The Lakota were ragged and hungry; they were short of ammunition and there was not enough game to feed everyone. The victories of the previous summer at the Rosebud and the Little Bighorn were now just memories. The army could absorb its losses; the Lakota and Cheyenne could not. They felt like hunted prey, with never a chance to rest. Under these circumstances, many people began to talk about giving up and returning to the reservation.

CRAZY HORSE BECOMES A DICTATOR

The Lakota had been at war since the summer. Crazy Horse was the war chief of the Oglala, but more importantly he was the inspirational leader of the two great victories at the Rosebud and the Little Bighorn. For that reason, he had enormous influence among the Lakota who were still at large. Crazy Horse's position was simple. He refused to compromise at all, especially after the murder of his peace delegation. He insisted on fighting the Americans to the end.

The "hostile" Lakota were irate when they learned that the reservation tribes had sold the "unceded" Powder River land. As a result, Crazy Horse and the council declared the Red Cloud Agency off-limits. The akicita forced families favoring surrender to stay with the hostiles. "One does not sell the earth upon which the people walk," said Crazy Horse.

Crazy Horse's stubbornness was acceptable to the people in August and September when the triumphs of the summer were recent memories. Now conditions were different. "A hard winter came on early," remembered one Lakota. "It snowed much; game was hard to find, and it was a hungry time for us. Ponies died, and we ate them." Still, Crazy Horse would not consider surrendering.

For a few months, Crazy Horse became almost a dictator. He tried to funnel all of the people's remaining resources to his supporters. He used his influence over the akicita to silence any talk of peace or surrender. Crazy Horse believed the Lakota needed to present a united front to resist. He felt it was impossible to fight if the Lakota drifted off, family by family, to the reservation.

In one case, Crazy Horse physically prevented people from leaving to go to the agency. He "shot all our horses," remembered one Lakota, "took our arms and knives, and all our plunder, and then told us if we wanted to go with the whites to go on, but the snow was so deep we could not travel without horses, and we had to return to the hostile camp." Most Lakota did not easily accept Crazy Horse's actions. Lakota society was very individualistic and democratic. Moderate leaders were horrified when Crazy Horse marched into other bands' villages and used his bodyguard to threaten people.

From Crazy Horse's perspective, the worst thing was that his extreme actions still did not stop people from surrendering in small groups. They were tired of starving, running from the soldiers, and seeing relatives die. One brief skirmish might use up the bullets that took several days of scrounging. There seemed to be no getting rid of the whites—there were too many of them.

WOLF MOUNTAIN

"Wherever we went, the soldiers came to kill us," said Black Elk, "and it was all our own country. It was ours already when the Wasichus made the treaty with Red Cloud that said it would be ours as long as the grass should grow and the water flow. That was only eight winters before, and they were chasing us now because we remembered and they forgot."

Crazy Horse had not given up hope. He believed he could lure Miles into one big fight that the Lakota could win. To do this, Crazy Horse led a series of small raids to draw Miles from his post. Miles took the bait and marched to the foothills of the Wolf Mountains in the Montana Territory. It was a grueling journey; the soldiers had to face harsh winds, subzero temperatures, deep snows, and frequent river crossings.

On January 8, 1877, Crazy Horse attacked Miles's soldiers about four miles southwest of present-day Birney along the Tongue River. In this Battle of Wolf Mountain, about 450 soldiers faced about 600 Lakota and Cheyenne warriors. Both sides hoped to win a decisive victory that would end the so-called Great Sioux War.

Miles set up a strong defensive position on a ridgeline. Early in the morning, Crazy Horse and Two Moons led a series of attacks but fell back before Army firepower. The Lakota regrouped several times. Miles was astonished to see Crazy Horse's warriors dismount and form what looked like firing lines. In his report, Miles stated that "they would leave their horses behind bluffs, and advance on foot, rifle in hand, filling every ravine and lining every crest. . . . This engagment [sic] was unlike any other Indian fight I ever witnessed, it was fought on ground . . . [and] not a single rifle being fired on horseback."

Crazy Horse's attempts to flank the American line also proved unsuccessful as Miles shifted his reserves to fill critical positions. Finally, the Lakota retired as a blizzard obscured the entire battlefield. The warriors withdrew up the Tongue River and Miles's soldiers returned to base, ending the winter campaign.

Both Miles and Crazy Horse wanted a decisive battle, but both would be disappointed. Five hours of fighting between the evenly matched adversaries left only about two dead on each side. Although technically a draw, the battle was a strategic victory for the U.S. Army. Crazy Horse had needed a victory. His group was starving, weakened by the winter, and faced with the enormous military power of the United States. A draw was not good enough to solve serious morale problems or the shortage of winter game.

SITTING BULL ARRIVES AND DEPARTS

One week after the battle, Sitting Bull arrived at Crazy Horse's camp. The Hunkpapa chief brought with him 100 lodges and a great deal of ammunition. Although Miles had pursued him across Montana, Sitting Bull still refused to surrender his weapons and report peacefully to the reservation.

The arrival of Sitting Bull temporarily cheered the Oglala, but it intensified the divisions between those who favored fighting and those who favored surrendering. Ironically, the Hunkpapa chief chose neither option. In February 1877, Sitting Bull led his followers to Canada rather than to submit to life on a reservation. There were still some buffalo left in Canada, and the pace of white settlement was much slower than in the United States. Neither Miles nor Crook could pursue Sitting Bull into Canada; the Canadian government would not allow it.

Crazy Horse considered this option, but he chose not to cross the border. Perhaps he did not want to leave his homeland. "My friend, the soldiers are everywhere," Crazy Horse told Sitting Bull. "This is the end. All the time these soldiers will keep hunting us down. Some day I shall be killed. Well, all right. I am going South to get mine." Sitting Bull quietly responded, "I do not wish to die yet." The two men who had led the Lakota resistance for the last seven years parted sadly. They would not meet again on this earth.

The news of Sitting Bull's flight to Canada stunned the few Lakota who wanted to continue their resistance. Sitting Bull's stubborn dislike for whites was as strong as Crazy Horse's. Crazy Horse began to accept the fact that he would not be able to live out his life as a free man. His objections to the Lakota who wished to surrender or negotiate began to soften. He began wandering off alone again. He knew there were just not enough warriors or supplies to defy another summer of army attacks. The party that supported armed resistance completely collapsed.

One day, Black Elk's father found Crazy Horse alone on a creek with just his wife. Crazy Horse explained to him, "Out there I am making plans—nothing but good plans—for the good of my people. This country is ours, therefore I am doing this."

HE HAS LOOKED
FOR DEATH . . .

General Crook did not like General Miles. Even though Crook was not in the field in early 1877, he was determined to get Crazy Horse's surrender. In February 1877, Crook sent Spotted Tail as his emissary to Crazy Horse. Spotted Tail was still an important Lakota chief and Crazy Horse's uncle as well. He told Crazy Horse that if he would surrender, Crook would see to it that the northern Lakota tribes received a reservation in the Powder River country.

By this time, most of the Lakota had no desire to continue the fight. Crook had a good reputation with Native Americans, not wholly deserved, as a man who tried to keep his promises. "You see all the people here are in rags," said Iron Hawk. "They all need clothing, we might as well go in." Crazy Horse said that whatever all the rest decided to do, he would do," recalled Red Feather. "So they all agreed to go in." Tired and hungry, the Lakota began the long journey from present-day Wyoming to northwestern Nebraska near the Red Cloud Agency.

On May 6, 1877, Crazy Horse led his people into Camp Robinson and shook the left hand of Lieutenant Philo Clark, General Crook's emissary at the fort and commander of the Indian scouts. "I shake with this hand because my heart is on this side," said Crazy

For the good of his people, Crazy Horse surrendered to U.S. troops on May 5, 1877. With 1,100 extremely cold, weak, and starving men, women, and children, Crazy Horse arrived at the Red Cloud Agency near Camp Robinson, Nebraska.

Horse. "I want this peace to last forever." As a sign of friendship, He Dog, a close ally of Crazy Horse, placed his own magnificent war bonnet and war shirt on the lieutenant's head and shoulders. The Great Sioux War was over.

Nevertheless, it was not a normal surrender. Crazy Horse entered the agency with 1,000 followers, two-thirds of whom were women and children, and more than 2,000 horses. The warriors rode in a procession with paint and feathers, carrying shields and weapons and singing songs. When the soldiers disarmed Crazy Horse's people, a thorough search turned up 114 weapons: 46 breechloaders, 35 muzzleloaders, and 33 revolvers. With these pathetic weapons, they had tried to fight off the entire U.S. Army.

Crook allowed the dignified surrender, and Philo Clark handled the situation extremely well. John Bourke noted, "There was no disorder, no bad feeling, which was remarkable enough considering that many of this band had never been on a Reserve before." In fact,

Bourke concluded, "If the Government will only keep its promises and treat these red men with justice, we shall have no more Indian wars."

"We all went in to the agency in good spirits," recalled Short Bull, and "there was no bad feeling among the chiefs or anybody." People were happy with the prospect of regular rations, a distribution of annuity goods, and reuniting with their relatives.

It is unlikely that Crazy Horse was in good spirits. John Bourke described him at the surrender as a man who "behaved with stolidity, like a man who saw he had to give in to fate, but would do so as doggedly as possible. . . . His face is quiet, rather morose, dogged, tenacious, and resolute. His expression is rather melancholic." According to one story, Crazy Horse said at the surrender, "All is lost anyway. . . . The country, the civilization the Indian enjoyed, and the freedom is lost."

FORT ROBINSON

"You see this barren waste," Red Cloud told a white visitor. "Think of it! I, who used to own rich soil in a well-watered country so extensive that I could not ride through it in a week on my fastest pony, am pout down here. . . . Now I, who used to control five thousand warriors, must tell Washington when I am hungry. I must beg for that which I own. If I beg hard, they put me in the guardhouse."

At the Red Cloud Agency, there were about 9,000 Oglala, 2,000 Cheyenne, and 1,500 Arapaho. At Spotted Tail's agency, there were 8,000 Brulés, 1,200 Minniconjou, and some Oglala. The two white Indian agents and their small staffs had an almost impossible time providing food and supplies for everyone. Both agencies had very few soldiers. They could not possibly keep track of everyone in the hilly, pine-covered land full of hidden valleys and unknown trails.

The last four months of Crazy Horse's life were the only four months that he was in contact with whites. Even then, he camped six miles from Fort Robinson and dealt with whites only when he could not avoid them. The white officers respected him for fighting them so hard in battle. This made the agency Lakota jealous. A rumor spread among the Lakota that the whites were going to make him chief of all the Lakota.

Yet the whites also did not trust him. Too many whites talked to him too much, and Crazy Horse had never really talked to white men before. He Dog said that "after a while Crazy Horse became so he did not want to go anywhere or talk to anyone." An American officer agreed that Crazy Horse was being "talked to too much, but if they would let him alone and not 'buzz' him so much he would come out all right."

The situation was not natural for Crazy Horse. All his life, he had been a warrior with little interest in politics, but everything on the reservation was politics. Crazy Horse would never master this game like Red Cloud. He could not make the adjustments required of him to become an agency Indian. He was often confused by what the whites expected of him and what he expected of himself. Many times, he must have thought about breaking away from the reservation and giving the warrior's life one final shot.

His presence at the agency created turbulence and tension among various factions of Lakota. None of the Lakota leaders were happy to see him. Crazy Horse projected the character of a warrior. Though the soldiers had forced him to come to the reservation, Crazy Horse had not been decisively defeated. Many reservation Lakota viewed him with jealousy and hatred. Just by existing, Crazy Horse challenged the authority of Red Cloud and Spotted Tail. In late June, the Lakota held a Sun Dance in Crazy Horse's honor. His dignity, reputation for spiritual power, and quiet refusal to bow to the whites who controlled the reservation all contributed to his aura.

He seemed optimistic at first. "Crazy Horse had come to the Agency with nothing but honorable intentions," said his friend Billy Garnett. For most of May 1877, "his frame of mind was tranquil and pacific." When he met General Crook, Crazy Horse kneeled before him, saying, "Three Stars, I have seen the white man. He is very strong. My heart is good." His gesture, the typical stance of a scout reporting to his chief, was a powerful sign of conciliation from Crazy Horse. There were other benefits to reservation life. The

Oglala were together and no longer starving. In addition, Dr. Valentine McGillycuddy offered to treat Black Shawl for her tuberculosis. He did treat her successfully; she lived until 1920.

CROOK'S PROMISES

General Crook made Crazy Horse two promises that he was later unwilling or unable to keep. He offered to get Crazy Horse an agency of his own in the Powder River country. He also promised the Lakota that they could leave the agency and go on a buffalo hunt.

These promises were crucial to Crazy Horse. He continually tried to unite the reservation Lakota to support a northern agency in the Black Hills. Sherman, Sheridan, and the Indian office, however, had already made the decision in Washington. They had decided to relocate all the Oglala along the Missouri River on land where the Lakota definitely did not want to live. As a soldier, Crook followed orders. He told Crazy Horse nothing about the impending move.

The buffalo hunt died a slower death. Crook at first supported the idea as a way to boost morale and give the formerly active Lakota something to do other than sitting around waiting for rations. Crook, however, soon had second thoughts. A buffalo hunt meant rearming the very same people he had just disarmed. Agency Lakota allied with Red Cloud told him that Crazy Horse was not to be trusted. He was "tricky" and "unfaithful," they said, and "very selfish." Gossip said that Crazy Horse would bolt the reservation as soon as he got hold of ammunition and horses. Crook decided it was better to cancel the buffalo hunt than to determine the depth of Crazy Horse's loyalty.

Instead, Crook tried to convince Crazy Horse to go to Washington, D.C. The trip to the East by Native American chiefs had been a basic part of American policy for a hundred years. The whites hoped that the Native leaders would be overawed by the enormity of white power, technology, and numbers.

Crazy Horse thought about going to Washington, but he insisted that Crook keep one of his promises before he went. Crazy Horse agreed to meet President Rutherford B. Hayes if he could have his agency or if there could be a buffalo hunt. After the cancellation of the buffalo hunt, Crazy Horse withdrew all support from the trip to Washington and refused to cooperate with the military and civilian agents. He ignored repeated invitations to attend the tribal council. Little Big Man and other leaders complained to the Indian agent that Crazy Horse's "dictatorial manners, and disregard for the comfort of his people" were causing great dissatisfaction among the Lakota. Whether by plan or not, Crazy Horse's actions were causing a crisis. Crook expressed increasing annoyance with Crazy Horse's lack of cooperation.

Crazy Horse began to suffer from mental and physical exhaustion. His mood swings became wider, ranging from deep depression to frenzied optimism.Unexpectedly, he took a second wife, a half-Cheyenne, half-French girl named Nellie Larrabee (sometimes spelled Laverie). The courtship apparently took place almost in secret. Many of Crazy Horse's followers disapproved of the match, but Black Shawl raised no objection if Crazy Horse wished to bring home a second wife. Nellie Larrabee became an important influence in the last month of his life. She increased Crazy Horse's fears by telling him that once in the government's power, he would be imprisoned and would never return.

THE NEZ PERCE

The Nez Perce were a Pacific Northwest tribe of no more than 7,000 members. They had warmly welcomed Lewis and Clark in 1805 and tried to cooperate with the United States, but gold rushes in the 1860s and 1870s brought miners and settlers illegally onto their lands. The U.S. government made a fraudulent treaty with a small part of the tribe that virtually gave the Americans 6 million acres (2.4 million hectares), nine-tenths of Nez Perce land.

In 1877, the U.S. government ordered the Nez Perce off their remaining land, promising them a reservation somewhere in Oregon. Although Chief Joseph and other chiefs prepared to leave peacefully, a skirmish broke out and people were killed. The fearful Nez Perce, totaling 750 men, women, and children, then began a masterful retreat toward Canada. The group covered 1,300 miles (2,092 km) in 75 days, all the while pursued by the U.S. Army. The Nez Perce fought 2,000 Regular Army troops and 18 Native American detachments in 18 separate engagements, winning two major battles at White Bird Canyon, Idaho, and Big Hole, Montana. The courage and tactical skill of the Nez Perce won an embarrassed admiration from the people of the Untied States.

General Crook was still enthusiastic about the use of Native American scouts. He sent a message to Crazy Horse asking if the Oglala warrior would fight against the Nez Perce. The request added to Crazy Horse's confusion. He had come to the reservation, given up his gun, and promised not to fight. Now the whites wanted to give him back his gun and fight the Nez Perce.

Crazy Horse was reluctant. After a long and very heated council on August 31, Crazy Horse appeared to agree. He told the whites that he was a man of peace, but if the whites insisted, he would keep fighting until all the Nez Perce were killed. Unfortunately, the translator distorted this to say that the war chief would fight until all the whites were killed. The reasons for the mistranslation, its actual impact, or even whether it really happened are still disputed.

The army was reconsidering the entire plan. They began to consider the folly of arming the one Lakota leader who was most likely to refuse to return to the agency. According to Philo Clark, Crazy Horse "told me he didn't intend to stay anymore and would leave at once . . . he did not like the country about here, that he never promised to stay here, and that he was going north with his band, that he had made up his mind and was certainly going."

Some time in midsummer of 1877, Americans such as Philo Clark and George Crook came to believe that the best thing to do with Crazy Horse was to arrest him and imprison him in Florida. They wanted him out of the way before he broke out and embarrassed everyone. It was clear that he was unhappy at the agency and that he missed the freedom of the Plains. Of all the Lakota, Crazy Horse clearly was the one most likely to fight again.

The majority of the Oglala people no longer supported Crazy Horse. They feared that he would misbehave and the government might react by immediately sending them off to the hated Missouri River Reservation. On September 2, more than 800 Oglala men attended a grand council to discuss the "problem" of Crazy Horse. Almost all of the most prominent leaders were there, including American Horse, Spotted Tail, and Red Cloud. American Horse announced that the elders had done their best to "quiet" Crazy Horse, hoping to "bring him into a better state of feeling" toward agency life; however, they could do "nothing with him" as "he had not attended our councils." They repeated the rumors that Crazy Horse was going to use the buffalo hunt or the scouting against the Nez Perce as an excuse to leave the reservation and resume hostilities with whites. After the council adjourned, Crook decided to restrict the freedom of Crazy Horse and his followers.

Friends of Crazy Horse supposedly went to Crook with the truth about the distorted translation. Crook started for Fort Robinson to talk to Crazy Horse. On the way, a Lakota troublemaker told Crook that Crazy Horse planned to kill him. There was such a climate of suspicion surrounding Crazy Horse at that time that Crook, usually not a fearful man, canceled the visit. Instead, he sent soldiers and the Oglala akicita to arrest Crazy Horse and bring him in.

THE ARREST OF CRAZY HORSE

Red Cloud, Spotted Tail, and their followers were determined to be rid of Crazy Horse. The Oglala band chiefs "all say Crazy Horse would not listen to them," observed a *New_York Tribune* reporter three days later. "He was obstinate, dictatorial, stubborn, and objected to every measure which was taken for their and his good." Many talked openly about killing Crazy Horse, "like a dog if he resisted," to get him out of the way.

On September 4, a huge force of soldiers and Indian police went to Crazy Horse's camp to arrest him, but he was not there. He had fled for the village of the Spotted Tail Agency, 40 miles (64 km) away. When Crazy Horse arrived, his uncle Spotted Tail was not happy to see him. Spotted Tail wanted no trouble, and Crazy Horse was a magnet for trouble. He was a symbol of resistance even when he was not resisting.

His pursuers caught up with him that night. Agent Jesse Lee, whom Crazy Horse trusted, spoke with him. Crazy Horse explained that he had offered to fight the Nez Perce, that he had not said anything about killing whites to the last man, that he did not intend to stab Crook in a council. Lee accepted Crazy Horse's explanations but told him that he would have to return to Fort Robinson and explain all this to General Bradley, the fort's commander. Crazy Horse replied, "I have been talked to night and day until my brain has turned." Lee insisted that Crazy Horse would be allowed to tell his side of the story.

Having no other option, Crazy Horse returned to Fort Robinson the next day. Lee said that Crazy Horse "seemed like a frightened, trembling, wild animal brought to bay, hoping for confidence one moment and fearing treachery the next. He had been under a severe nervous strain all day and it plainly showed."

A FATEFUL DEATH

Unlike the rest of his life, Crazy Horse's death is well documented. In fact, more has been written about the last day of his life than the other 37 years of his life put together. There were many witnesses; however, their accounts differ greatly in matters of detail and sometimes even contradict each other on important points.

It is not disputed that on September 5, 1877, Crazy Horse rode into Fort Robinson. Thousands of Lakota assembled; there was not much to do on the agency and the situation promised high drama. A path opened for Crazy Horse. He had time to say a few words to He Dog before walking with Agent Lee to what he thought would be his promised interview with General Bradley. It was about 6 P.M.

General Bradley, however, did not intend to see Crazy Horse. Bradley's orders were clear: Crazy Horse was to be arrested and shipped immediately to Omaha and then to prison in Florida. Lee's promise that Crazy Horse could get a hearing from General Bradley turned out to be one more American lie. Instead, Little Big Man,

This painting by Amos Bad Heart Buffalo depicts what some people believe happened to Crazy Horse. It shows a sergeant and Indian policeman holding Crazy Horse by the arms while a soldier stabs him with a bayonet.

now a member of the Indian police, and Lieutenant Kensington (the officer of the day) led Crazy Horse past an office to the guardhouse.

From here, accounts tend to differ widely. Apparently, the moment Crazy Horse saw the filthy cells with the chained prisoners, he knew he had been betrayed. "I won't go in there," Crazy Horse said flatly. Behind him, the hammers of rifles clicked but no shot was fired. Crazy Horse began to resist. He whirled and attempted to run back into the parade ground of the fort. He was just clear of the door when Little Big Man jumped on his back and tried to grab his arms. The Lakota on the parade ground could see the forms of the two men. Many of them were, at this moment, hostile to Crazy Horse and shouting, "Kill him, kill him."

Crazy Horse had managed to conceal a knife under his blanket. He finally got one arm free and cut Little Big Man. The pain made Little Big Man loosen his grip. For a moment, it looked like Crazy

Horse might break free and make a fight of it. Then, a 47-year-old white private, William Gentles, ran forward and bayoneted Crazy Horse once or twice. A thrust punctured his lung, causing Crazy Horse to sink down, his blood seeping into the dust of the parade ground.

Later, Little Big Man and American Horse insisted that Crazy Horse had accidentally stabbed himself as he struggled to break free. Accounts of the other witnesses, however, agree that Little Big Man tried to hold him, that many were ready to shoot him, that other Lakota grabbed him, and that Gentiles stabbed him. There is a famous pictographic record of the stabbing done by Amos Bad Heart Bull in which Crazy Horse's arms are held by his own people, just as his vision so long ago supposedly promised.

After Crazy Horse's stabbing, there was absolute chaos in the room and on the parade ground. Everyone was tense and confused. Supporters and opponents of Crazy Horse were one gunshot away from killing each other in a major riot. Then, they remembered the bleeding Crazy Horse. Technically, he was still supposed to be imprisoned in the guardhouse, but Dr. McGillycuddy convinced a reluctant General Bradley to put him in an adjutant's office. Once in the office, Crazy Horse refused a cot and was placed on the floor. The doctor gave him morphine to ease the pain, and he died at about midnight on September 6, 1877.

Crazy Horse's last words are not clear and there are many stories. Some witnesses say he made a long speech as he lay mortally wounded. This seems unlikely, for Crazy Horse was a quiet man and not the type who would give a deathbed oration. Others say Crazy Horse spoke to his father, Worm, who was with him: "Father, I am hurt bad. It is no good for the people to depend on me any longer."

When dawn broke, Worm sat near his son's lifeless body. So, too, did Touch the Clouds, who supposedly said, "It is good. He has looked for death, and it has come." Dr. McGillycuddy called his death "a combination of treachery, jealousy, and unreliable reports resulted in a 'frame-up' and he was railroaded to his death." Black Elk came to the same conclusion from the perspective of a Lakota supporter. "Crazy Horse was dead," said Black Elk. "He was brave and good and wise. He never wanted anything but to save his people, and he fought the Wasichus only when they came to kill us in our own country.... They could not kill him in battle. They had to lie to him and kill him that way."

HARD TIMES HAVE COME ON US

Indian Bureau officials and Army officers feared that Crazy Horse's death might lead to violence from his followers. That night, many of the vastly outnumbered white people in Fort Robinson expected to be killed. Despite the tension, however, the spirit was temporarily gone from the Lakota and the night passed without incident. "Everything is quiet," wrote John Bourke in his diary, "and I think will remain so. Crazy Horse's body was brought to the agency and put on a little platform, Indian fashion, on the hill overlooking the post, not half a mile away."

Crazy Horse's parents were crushed. His mother and father sang the death song until early morning. They took the body, wrapped it in a blanket, lashed it to a travois (a frame used for dragging loads), and carried it to Spotted Tail's agency. There, they placed the body on a small scaffold about a half mile above Camp Sheridan. "We were not agency Indians," Worm wailed. "We preferred the buffalo to the white man's beef, but the Gray Fox [Crook] kept sending messengers to us in the north, saying come in, come in. Well, we came in, and now they have killed my boy; hard times have come upon us...."

A month later, General Crook moved the Lakota to their new smaller agencies. As the Lakota suspected, it was not in the Black Hills or the Powder River country but on land they hated near the Missouri River. Sometime during the trip, Crazy Horse's parents slipped away from the main group and buried his body. "The old people never would tell where they took the body of their son," said Black Elk. "Nobody knows today where he lies, for the old people are dead too." Legend has it that the site is close to Wounded Knee Creek, near the site of the horrible Wounded Knee Massacre of the Lakota in 1890.

END OF
THE OLD LIFE

Although Crazy Horse died in 1877, no account of his life can end without mentioning the Dawes Act (1887) and the Wounded Knee Massacre (1890). They represent the final chapter in his life story—the destruction of the old Lakota way of life and the lowest point of Lakota history in North America.

The Dawes Act came about because some well-intentioned reformers argued against segregating Native Americans on reservations. Instead, they believed that Native Americans could achieve economic prosperity if they embraced private property. They argued that the communal values of the tribes prevented the pursuit of personal success that lay at the heart of capitalism.

To force such values on Native Americans, the U.S. Congress passed the Dawes Act in 1887 over the strenuous objections of leaders such as Red Cloud and Sitting Bull. The Dawes Act dissolved community-owned tribal lands and granted "allotments" to individual families according to size. The Dawes Act also awarded citizenship, after a 25-year waiting period, to all Native Americans who accepted their land, lived apart from the tribe, and adopted the habits of "civilized life." Whites planned to use education, land policy, and federal law to do away with tribal society forever. Greedy

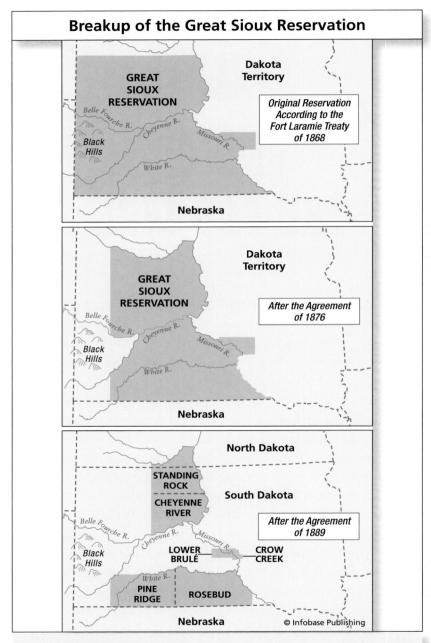

Breakup of the Great Sioux Reservation

This map shows the reductions in Sioux land after only 20 years. Following the Dawes Allotment Act, the remaining reservations were greatly reduced even more. In less than 50 years, tribal ownership dropped from 154 million acres (in 1887) to 48 million acres (in 1934).

western ranchers, railroaders, settlers, and land speculators all backed the bill because it would free up millions of acres of "surplus land" for land-hungry whites.

The Dawes Act destroyed the Native Americans' tribal structure and their ability to control the land. Tribal land ownership dropped from 154 million acres (62 million ha) in 1887 to 78 million (31 million ha) in 1900 to 48 million (19 ha) in 1934 (when the law was repealed). By the Great Depression, two-thirds of Native Americans in the United States lacked any property.

The act had particularly disastrous consequences for the Lakota. When South Dakota became a state in 1889, white settlers pressured the federal government to break up the Great Sioux Reservation into four separate reservations: Pine Ridge (Oglala), Rosebud (Brulé), Standing Rock (Hunkpapa), and Cheyenne River (Minneconjou). In complete violation of the Second Treaty of Fort Laramie, the government reduced the Lakota reservation by half and gave the remaining lands in South Dakota to whites. By 1934, the Rosebud Reservation alone had lost an additional 2 million acres of its original territory.

WOUNDED KNEE AND THE END OF NATIVE RESISTANCE

In 1889, the Lakota were in desperate straits. They had lost their land, the buffalo were gone, and their way of life was under constant attack by the U.S. government. On shrinking reservations, Native Americans depended on government rations and annual payments stipulated by treaties. This allowed government agents of the Bureau of Indian Affairs to control tribal life by threatening to withhold rations. When the rations were issued, they were often insufficient and very poor in quality. The government refused to honor agreements such as providing farming equipment and livestock. Indian agents stole the annuity payments that the Lakota were entitled to or gave them out selectively. None of this was in dispute; it was simply that the whites did not care.

In 1889, many northern tribes turned to a mystical religion based on a "Ghost Dance" taught to them by Wovoka, a Paiute religious leader. The sacred Ghost Dance, if done properly, promised that whites would disappear and living and dead Native Americans would be reunited to live free from death, disease, and misery. The Ghost Dance spread rapidly across the Plains, captivating the Lakota, the Cheyenne, and the Arapaho. One Oglala Lakota said, "The people were hungry and in despair, and many believed in the good new world that was coming."

The Ghost Dance unnerved Indian agents and Army officers. Thousands of Lakota at all four reservations refused the orders to stop dancing. The Pine Ridge Indian agent wrote, "Indians are dancing in the snow and are wild and crazy. . . . We need protection, and we need it now. The leaders should be arrested and confined in some military post until the matter is quieted, and this should be done at once."

Sitting Bull had returned to the United States in 1881 and was living at the Standing Rock Reservation at the time. Sitting Bull expressed support for the Ghost Dance movement, which he saw as a way to resist white authority. On December 14, 1890, Indian police killed Sitting Bull while he was supposedly "resisting arrest." The murder strengthened the belief of the Lakota that a great massacre was imminent.

Two weeks later, the U.S. Army surrounded a band of Lakota at the Wounded Knee settlement of the Pine Ridge Reservation. When a small skirmish broke out, the American soldiers fired mercilessly into the encampment, including the use of the newly invented machine gun. Within minutes, the army had slaughtered more than 140 men, women, and children; the actual number is probably closer to 300. In 1990, the U.S. Congress passed a resolution recognizing the incident at Wounded Knee as a massacre (and not a "battle") and issued a statement of deep regret.

In his old age, Black Elk, the Lakota medicine man, reflected on the massacre at Wounded Knee. "I did not know then how much was ended," he said. "When I look back now from this high hill of my old age, I can still see the butchered women and children lying heaped and scattered all along the crooked gulch as plain as when I saw them with eyes still young. And I can see that something else died there in the bloody mud, and was buried in the blizzard. A people's dream died there. It was a beautiful dream . . . the nation's hoop is broken and scattered. There is no center any longer, and the sacred tree is dead."

The Buffalo Soldiers

The Lakota regularly used the term "white man" as a synonym for "American." In the same way, many historians freely use the term "white people" to describe the adversaries of Native Americans. Yet some of the best U.S. soldiers had dark skin. African-American soldiers had fought in the Revolution and the War of 1812, and 200,000 had served in the Civil War. After 1865, the U.S. government organized the black soldiers who wanted to remain in the army into the 9th and 10th Cavalry Regiments. For the next 20 years, these "Buffalo Soldiers" battled Native Americans from Montana to Arizona.

The reason they received the name "Buffalo Soldiers" is uncertain. It is possible that Native tribes were comparing the black soldiers' hair to the mane of a buffalo. Another view is that a wounded buffalo will fight ferociously and courageously. Either way, the name was probably an honor since the Plains tribes held the buffalo in such high regard.

The Buffalo Soldiers did most of their fighting against the Comanche, Ute, and Apache in the Southwest. They also built forts and roads, installed telegraph lines, guarded water holes, escorted wagon trains, and protected stagecoaches.

The Buffalo Soldiers were also present after the massacre at Wounded Knee and fought to force Lakota warriors back to the reservation. Individual black soldiers might have sympathized with the Lakota, but they were employed to fight Native Americans. The Buffalo Soldiers and their officers did not make Indian policy; they carried it out, regardless of merit, to the best of their ability.

With the massacre at Wounded Knee, armed resistance by Native Americans to the white invasion ended. The Lakota suffered from apathy, hopelessness, hunger, and disease. The buffalo were gone and the old life of nomadic hunting and raiding disappeared completely. The Lakota of 1860 were affluent and independent. Hardly a generation later, the Lakota were nearly landless and dependent on the U.S. government.

THE LAKOTA TODAY

In 1900, census takers counted only 237,000 Native Americans in the United States, reduced from an estimated 5 million in 1492. Most whites believed that Native Americans were a "vanishing race" incapable of civilization, unable to accept assimilation, and doomed to inevitable extinction.

Many tribes, however, made a remarkable recovery in the twentieth century. The 2000 census showed that the U.S. population was 281 million; of that number, 4.1 million, or 1.5 percent, reported they were of American Indian or Alaskan Native ancestry, and the number is growing rapidly. The assumptions of white Americans in the 1800s have turned out to be very wrong.

Most of the descendants of Crazy Horse, Red Cloud, and Sitting Bull live today in South Dakota. Like the members of all ethnic groups, they range in character from the virtuous to the unscrupulous, with most members falling somewhere in between. Many Lakota have become successful professionals while others live in poverty. No one is alive anymore who can personally remember the great victories over the army of the United States at the Rosebud and the Little Bighorn.

According to the 2000 census, the Lakota population of the United States was 153,000. This placed them fifth among the largest Native American tribal groupings, behind the Cherokee, Navajo, Latin American Indian, and Choctaw. Today, about half of all Lakota live on reservations in North and South Dakota, Montana, and Minnesota and also in Manitoba and Saskatchewan in Canada.

The Lakota are no longer aggressive nomads who roam across the Great Plains. Instead, like most modern-day Americans, the

One way the Lakota continue to honor their ancestors is with the annual Big Foot Memorial Ride, a two-week horse ride that retraces the final journey of Chief Big Foot and his band before they were killed at Wounded Knee. Here, Chief Arvol Looking Horse, nineteenth generation Keeper of the Sacred White Buffalo Pipe leads groups of Lakota on the ride in South Dakota.

Lakota struggle to perform the careful balancing act of preserving the best parts of their traditional culture while facing the challenges of the twenty-first century. They try to keep their land, to seek justice for their people, and to maintain a harmonious community life.

The Lakota experienced a renaissance in the second half of the 1900s. There was a renewal of traditional religion, ceremonies, and healing practices. The tribe developed better ways to deal with the federal government, greater freedom over their own tribal affairs, and increasing independence for off-reservation people. Lakota festivals celebrating their history and culture are now crucial parts of the South Dakota economy.

Most of Crazy Horse's people live on the Pine Ridge Oglala Lakota Indian Reservation. Pine Ridge is in the southwest corner of South Dakota, 50 miles east of the Wyoming border. The 3,400 square-mile (9,000-sq km) reservation is the second-largest Native American reservation in the United States. The number of people who live at Pine Ridge is controversial; estimates range from 15,000 to 40,000.

A number of long-standing problems have persisted at Pine Ridge. In 2009, the median income on the reservation was less than $4,000 per year, while unemployment was more than 80 percent. About 97 percent of the population of Pine Ridge lives below poverty levels, and housing is often wretched. Many people suffer from health problems. The infant mortality rate on the reservation is the highest on this continent, and almost half of the adults over the age of 40 have diabetes. Alcoholism affects 8 out of 10 families at Pine Ridge.

The Oglala Lakota, however, are a determined, proud, and adaptable people. They are working hard to overcome the problems on the reservation. They are continuing to work to reclaim their self-sufficiency and culture, and once again create a new way of life.

MANIFEST DESTINY IN REVERSE

In the late 1800s, Americans thought the Great Plains was valuable agricultural land. When the buffalo and the Native Americans disappeared, whites moved to the Plains in great numbers. There was plenty of rain on the prairie in the late 1800s and early 1900s, and farms flourished; however, years of drought followed, and homesteaders began to leave. The ruins of their farms dot the rural Plains.

The area has experienced massive population loss over the last 80 years. The counties of the rural Plains, which experienced a peak in population in 1920, have lost more than a half million people—a third of their population—since then. Several hundred thousand square miles of the Great Plains have fewer than six persons per square mile, and large areas have fewer than two persons per square mile. According to the 2000 census, 272 of the 443 Plains counties have experienced population declines since 1990, and the declines are accelerating. Deaths vastly exceed births, schools are closing, and families are selling their farms.

The decline has particularly affected North and South Dakota. North Dakota had 647,000 people in 1920 and only 642,000 in 2000. Thirty of South Dakota's counties lost population between the 1990 and the 2000 census. Scholars estimate that rural counties of the Dakotas could lose an additional third of their population over the next 20 years.

In recent years, there has been serious discussion about one day turning large areas of the Great Plains into a vast nature preserve. Some people want to return thousands of square miles to Native prairie and reintroduce the buffalo that once grazed there. The area would then become a vast, government-owned "Buffalo Commons," used for tourism and the production of buffalo-related products. The buffalo has become one of the conservation movement's great success stories. Rescued from the brink of extinction in 1900, buffalo now number more than 400,000 and are no longer considered endangered.

Some Native American people believe that the Plains were not totally "lost." After all, Native tribes lived there for more than a thousand years while Americans have only been on the Plains for little more than a century. Perhaps the Lakota and Cheyenne will ultimately outlast the white occupation of the Plains, just as they lived through other periods of hardship and misfortune.

IN THE SPIRIT OF CRAZY HORSE

To the white Americans of the late 1800s, Crazy Horse was a merciless and savage murderer. John Bourke, generally sympathetic to Native Americans, described Crazy Horse as "a villainous old rascal" who "particularly adhered to a career of spoilation and murder." Yet when Crazy Horse surrendered, Bourke had to concede, "All Indians give him [Crazy Horse] a high reputation for courage and generosity. In advancing upon an enemy, none of his warriors were allowed to pass him. He had made hundreds of friends by his charity toward the poor, as it was a point of honor with him never to keep anything for himself, excepting weapons of war. I never heard an Indian mention his name in any save terms of respect."

In the twenty-first century, the latter image of Crazy Horse has triumphed. He is most frequently portrayed as a man who valiantly defended his people against the invasion of the United States into Lakota tribal lands. Generals George Crook and Nelson Miles are barely remembered anymore. Yet the leaders of the Native tribes they tried to grind into dust—Sitting Bull and Crazy Horse—remain alive in American culture. In South Dakota, the enormous Crazy Horse Memorial dwarfs the nearby, little town of Custer, named after his old adversary.

As a leader, Crazy Horse kept the interests of his people before his own. He provided for them and protected them from harm. He signed no treaties and surrendered only because he did not want to see his followers suffer from starvation and cold. "He was a great man," said Black Elk, "and they could not kill him in battle and he would not make himself over into a Wasichu, as Spotted Tail and the others did."

Native people, and all Americans, continue to be inspired by Crazy Horse's honor and courage, generosity and strength. It is appropriate that the words most closely associated with him is the Lakota war cry *"hoka hey."* This can be translated several ways, such as "Today is a good day to die," "Hold fast," "Take courage," or just "Charge." All translations seem to capture the optimistic fatalism of the Lakota warrior spirit.

When Native Americans fought for their rights and preached pride in their heritage in the 1960s, it is not surprising that they fixed upon Crazy Horse as a symbol of dignity, self-esteem, and resistance. The spirit of Crazy Horse remained unbroken in the 1800s and it remains unbroken today. He is a hero, not only to Native Americans but also to all Americans who prize freedom and honor.

CHRONOLOGY

1600–1700 Horses spread from the Southwest across the Plains.

c. 1840 Crazy Horse is born.

1848 Mexican-American War ends.

1849 California Gold Rush begins.

1851 The first Treaty of Fort Laramie is signed on September 17. The United States negotiates with the Plains Indians to guarantee safe passage for settlers on the Oregon Trail in return for payment of $50,000 each year for 50 years.

1862 In the Dakota War of 1862 (also called the Dakota Conflict or Sioux Uprising), the Dakota battle American settlers and later the U.S. Army over treaty violations. On December 26, thirty-eight Dakota are hanged in the largest one-day execution in American history.

1864 On November 29, a 700-man militia from Colorado Territory kill and mutilate more than 100 Cheyenne and Arapaho (mostly women and children) in their village. This incident is now known as the Sand Creek Massacre.

1865 Crazy Horse is honored with the title of Shirt Wearer.

1866–1868   The Lakota, Cheyenne, and Arapaho fight the United States for control of the Powder River Country and the Bozeman Trail in north-central Wyoming. Called Red Cloud's War, it is named after the prominent Oglala Lakota chief, Red Cloud.

1868   The second Treaty of Fort Laramie is signed on April 29. It guarantees the Sioux ownership of the Black Hills and further land and hunting rights in South Dakota, Wyoming, and Montana, and ends Red Cloud's War. The Bozeman Trail is closed and U.S. forts are abandoned.

1869   The world's first transcontinental railroad is completed. It is a vital link for trade, commerce,

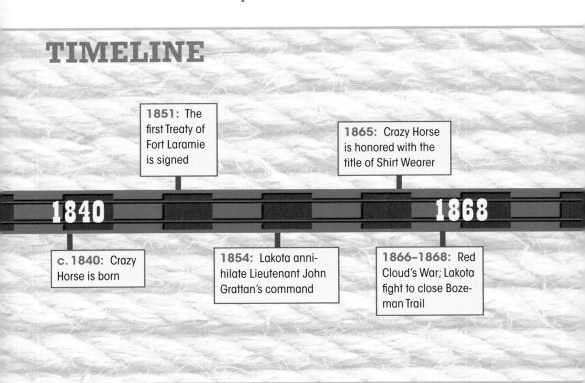

TIMELINE

1851: The first Treaty of Fort Laramie is signed

1865: Crazy Horse is honored with the title of Shirt Wearer

1840

1868

c. 1840: Crazy Horse is born

1854: Lakota annihilate Lieutenant John Grattan's command

1866–1868: Red Cloud's War; Lakota fight to close Bozeman Trail and travel between the eastern and the western United States.

1870   Crazy Horse elopes with Black Buffalo Woman, who is already married to No Water. No Water shoots Crazy Horse in the jaw, and later must pay Crazy Horse three horses for his injury. Crazy Horse resigns his title as Shirt Wearer.

Crazy Horse marries Black Shawl. They later have a daughter, They Are Afraid of Her. She dies of cholera at age 3.

1871   The Red Cloud Agency is established on the Platte River in Wyoming Territory.

1868: The second Treaty of Fort Laramie is signed; Bozeman Trail is closed; forts are abandoned

1876: The Great Sioux War begins; Crazy Horse checks Crooks advance at the Rosebud; Crazy Horse helps annihilate Custer's command at Little Bighorn

1868

1877

1870: Crazy Horse elopes with Black Buffalo Woman; Crazy Horse marries Black Shawl

1877: Crazy Horse surrenders, Crazy Horse is killed

1876   Thousands of miners flood into the Black Hills to find gold, although this is in violation of the second Laramie treaty. A series of battles between the United States and the Lakota and Cheyenne, called the Great Sioux War, begins.

Battle of the Rosebud is fought on June 17 for control of the Black Hills. Crazy Horse leads a group of Lakota and Cheyenne in a surprise attack against General George Crook's forces. This delays Crook from joining with General George Custer's 7th Cavalry.

Battle of Little Big Horn is fought on June 25. Crazy Horse helps annihilate Custer's command at Little Bighorn

1877   Crazy Horse and his warriors fight their last battle at Wolf Mountain on January 8, ending the Great Sioux War. Weak, cold, and hungry, he and his people surrender at Camp Robinson in Nebraska.

At council, on August 31, Crazy Horse agrees to help the U.S. Army in their war against the Nez Perce. His words are misinterpreted to mean he would fight until all the whites are killed. General Crook orders Crazy Horse's arrest, and Crazy Horse is killed during a struggle on September 6.

1887   U.S. Congress passes the Dawes Act on February 8, calling for the division of tribal lands into individual parcels.

1890   Sitting Bull is killed.

Wounded Knee massacre at Pine Ridge Reservation occurs.

GLOSSARY

akicita   A Lakota warrior society that policed Lakota villages.

assimilation   The blending of minority groups into the dominant society. White Americans in the 1800s offered the Lakota the choice of assimilation or extermination.

Battle of the Little Bighorn   Famous battle in eastern Montana fought on June 25, 1876, between the U.S. Army under George Custer and the Sioux and Cheyenne led by Crazy Horse and Sitting Bull. The Lakota won a complete tactical victory, although the triumph had little strategic outcome on the Sioux War of 1876–1877.

Battle of the Rosebud   Six-hour battle in the Montana Territory on June 17, 1876, fought between evenly numbered forces of the U.S. Army under George Crook and the Lakota led by Crazy Horse. At the end, the U.S. Army held the field but the Lakota had won the tactical victory.

Black Hills   Small mountain range in western South Dakota and eastern Wyoming. The Treaty of Fort Laramie (1868) awarded the Black Hills to the Lakota; the United States' violation of the treaty led to the Sioux War of 1876–1877.

Bozeman Trail   Overland route connecting the gold fields of Montana to the Oregon Trail. The flow of whites through Lakota territory from 1863 to 1865 led to Red Cloud's War of 1866–1868.

Buffalo Soldiers   Native American nickname for several African American cavalry units who fought in the American West in the late 1800s. They participated in several encounters with the Lakota.

Camp Robinson   Military encampment of the U.S. government at the Red Cloud Agency. Sometimes known as Fort Robinson.

company   Military unit of approximately 50 to 200 soldiers. Most companies consisted of two to five platoons.

coup   Basis of complex rules of bravery that motivated most Plains Indian warfare. The most prestigious act was to directly risk death by attacking or even touching an enemy at close range and then getting away safely. This was known as "counting coup."

Dawes Act   Action by U.S. Congress in 1887 to assimilate Native Americans by replacing tribal landholdings with individual allotments. The act was a disaster for Native Americans; whites used the Dawes Act to steal the vast majority of tribal land in the American West.

ethnocentric   Belief in the superiority of one's own ethnic group.

Fetterman Fight   Battle on December 21, 1866, between the U.S. Army and the Lakota, Cheyenne, and Arapaho. Crazy Horse's leadership helped wipe out William Fetterman's entire command in a brilliant ambush near Fort Phil Kearny in Wyoming.

Ghost Dance   Religious dance of Native Americans hoping for communication with the dead and the coming of an Indian messiah who would make the whites disappear. The Paiute prophet Wovoka spread the Ghost Dance to the Lakota in 1889, and the ritual played a role in leading to the Wounded Knee Massacre.

Great Plains   Imprecise area between the Mississippi River and the Rocky Mountains (about 500 miles or 800 kilometers) and extending from Canada to southern Texas (about 2,000 miles or 3,200 kilometers). The Lakota lived in the lush grasslands of the Northern Plains.

Lakota   Largest of the three groups that made up the Sioux nation (along with the Dakota and Nakota). The Lakota consisted of a loose confederation of seven subgroups: the Oglala, Brulé,

Minniconjou, Sans Arc, Blackfoot Lakota, Two Kettles, and Hunkpapa.

manifest destiny   Belief by American whites in the 1800s that the United States was chosen by God to extend across the continent and beyond. The term served as the justification for American expansionism and imperialism.

Oglala   One of the main regional branches of the Lakota. Crazy Horse was a member of this group.

pemmican   Tough buffalo meat that was dried and pounded together with fat and wild berries. It was a nutritious food that could be easily carried and eaten on the trail.

Pine Ridge Reservation   Current Oglala reservation (about 5,600 square miles or 9,000 square kilometers) located in the southwest corner of South Dakota on the Nebraska border. It was established in 1889 and was the site of the Wounded Knee Massacre.

Powder River country   Area of the Great Plains in northeastern Wyoming between the Bighorn Mountains and the Black Hills. It was the center of Lakota hunting territory in the 1860s and 1870s and the focus of Red Cloud's War.

rations   Portions assigned to a person or group. By treaty, the Lakota were often entitled to food, clothing, and other rations in exchange for their cooperation or the "sale" of their land.

Red Cloud Agency   Native reservation located in northwestern Nebraska. Crazy Horse surrendered there (May 1877) and was killed there (September 1877).

Red Cloud's War   Conflict from 1866 to 1868 fought between the United States and Native Americans in the Wyoming and Montana Territories. The Second Treaty of Fort Laramie (1868) temporarily preserved Lakota control of the Powder River country.

reservation   Area that is reserved for a specific purpose. In the 1800s, the U.S. government set aside specific areas reserved for Native Americans and tried to force most Native Americans to live there.

Sand Creek Massacre   Unprovoked surprise attack by the Colorado militia on a peaceful Cheyenne and Arapaho village on November 29, 1864. They murdered more than 100 Native Americans. The attack helped convince the Cheyenne to join the Lakota in resisting white expansion.

scalping   Removal of all or part of the scalp, usually with hair attached, from an enemy's head. In the late 1800s, Native Americans and whites often scalped the bodies of their dead enemies.

Sun Dance   Important Native American ritual celebrated by almost all Plains Indians. The ceremony usually took place in summer, often over several days, and attempted to revive the mysterious powers that ensured the Native Americans' welfare.

telegraph   Electrical device for sending and receiving messages over long distances. It became popular in the United States in the 1840s. For most of the 1800s, it was the only way to convey information quickly over very long distances.

Treaty of Fort Laramie (1851)   Agreement between major Native American tribes on the Northern Plains and the U.S. government. The Lakota received the area north of the Platte and west of the Missouri and pledged they would not attack travelers crossing their territory on the Oregon Trail. In exchange, the U.S. government agreed to pay the tribes $50,000 each year for 50 years (later reduced by the U.S. Senate to 10 years).

Treaty of Fort Laramie (1868)   Agreement between the Lakota and the U.S. government that concluded Red Cloud's War. The treaty recognized the Lakota victory; the United States abandoned the Bozeman Trail and all forts on Lakota territory, gave the Lakota ownership of the western half of South Dakota, and reserved the Powder River country "for the absolute and undisturbed use and occupation" of the Lakota.

tribe   Social group made up of many families, clans, or generations. Tribal members usually share values and organize themselves for mutual care and defense.

vision quest   Common rite of passage in Plains Indian culture. A person would go into the wilderness to seek a vision. A successful quest produced a contact with a supernatural guide who could solve a problem or possibly even reveal the future.

wakan   Mysterious force believed by the Lakota to be present in everything in the world. People had the ability to acquire wakan power in several ways, such as the vision quest or the Sun Dance.

wasichus   Lakota term, often derogatory, for white Americans.

Wounded Knee Massacre   Attack on December 29, 1890, by U.S. Army troops on a Lakota encampment at Pine Ridge Reservation in South Dakota. At least 140 Native Americans were killed, including many women and children. The incident is often considered the end of the "Indian wars" of the 1800s.

BIBLIOGRAPHY

Aleshire, Peter. *The Fox and the Whirlwind: General George Crook and Geronimo, A Paired Biography*. New York: John Wiley & Sons, 2000.

Ambrose, Stephen. *Crazy Horse and Custer: The Parallel Lives of Two American Warriors*. New York: Doubleday, 1975.

"American Indian and Alaska Native Population—2000." Census 2000 Brief. Available online. URL: http://74.125.45.132/search?q=cache:TLyJ_se-hSoJ:www.census.gov/prod/2002pubs/c2kbr01-15.pdf+census+native+americans+2000+percentage&cd=1&hl=en&ct=clnk&gl=us&ie=UTF-8.

Andrist, Ralph. *The Long Death: The Last Days of the Plains Indians*. Norman: University of Oklahoma Press, 2001.

Bancroft-Hunt, Norman. *The Indians of the Great Plains*. New York: Peter Bedrick, 1989.

Banner, Stuart. *How the Indians Lost Their Land: Law and Power on the Frontier*. Cambridge, Mass.: Harvard University Press, 2005.

Beck, Paul. *The First Sioux War: The Grattan Fight and Blue Water Creek 1854–1856*. Lanham, Md.: University Press of America, 2004.

Bonvillain, Nancy. *The Teton Sioux*. New York: Chelsea House, 1994.

Bourke, John. *On the Border with Crook*. New York: Scribner's, 1891.

Bray, Kingsley. *Crazy Horse: A Lakota Life*. Norman: University of Oklahoma Press, 2006.

Carlson, Paul. *The Plains Indians*. College Station: Texas A&M University Press, 1998.

Chacon, Richard and David Dye, eds. *The Taking and Displaying of Human Body Parts as Trophies by Amerindians*. New York: Springer, 2007.

Clark, Robert. *The Killing of Chief Crazy Horse*. Glendale, Calif.: Arthur Clark, 1976.

Connell, Evan. *Son of the Morning Star*. San Francisco: North Point, 1984.

Crazy Horse Memorial. Available online. URL: http://www.crazyhorsememorial.org/.

Crook, George. *General George Crook: His Autobiography*. Schmitt, Martin (ed.). Norman: University of Oklahoma Press, 1946.

Custer, George. *My Life on the Plains; or, Personal Experiences with Indians*. Norman: University of Oklahoma Press, 1962 [1874].

"The Dakota Conflict Trials, 1862," Famous American Trials—University of Missouri-Kansas City School of Law. Available online at http://www.law.umkc.edu/faculty/projects/ftrials/dakota/dakota.html.

Donovan, James. *A Terrible Glory: Custer and the Little Bighorn—The Last Great Battle of the American West*. New York: Little, Brown, 2008.

Doyle, Susan. *Journeys to the Land of Gold*. Helena: Montana Historical Society, 2000.

Flores, Dan. "Bison Ecology and Bison Diplomacy: The Southern Plains, 1800–1850." *Journal of American History* 78 (1991): 465-85.

Fox, Richard Allen, Jr. *Archaeology, History, and Custer's Last Battle: The Little Big Horn Reexamined*. Norman: University of Oklahoma Press, 1993.

Freedman, Russell. *The Life and Death of Crazy Horse*. New York: Holiday House, 1996.

Graham, W.A. *The Custer Myth: A Source Book of Custeriana*. Harrisburg, Pa.: Stackpole Company, 1953.

Gray, John. *Custer's Last Campaign: Mitch Boyer and the Little Big Horn Reconstructed*. Lincoln: University of Nebraska Press, 1991.

Greene, Jerome. *Evidence and the Custer Enigma: A Reconstruction of Indian-Military History*. Golden, Colo.: Outbooks, 1986 [1973].

Hammer, Kenneth. *Custer in '76: Walter Camp's Notes on the Custer Fight*. Provo, Utah: Brigham Young University Press, 1976.

Hassrick, Royal. *The Sioux: Life and Customs of a Warrior Society*. Norman: University of Oklahoma Press, 1982 [1964].

Hoebel, E. Adamson. *The Cheyennes: Indians of the Great Plains*. New York: Holt, Rinehart, and Winston, 1960.

Hoig, Stan. *The Battle of the Washita*. Lincoln: University of Nebraska Press, 1976.

Hoxie, Frederick, ed. *Encyclopedia of North American Indians*. Boston: Houghton Mifflin, 1996.

Hyde, George. *Red Cloud's Folk: A History of the Oglala Sioux Indians*. Norman: University of Oklahoma Press, 1937.

_____. *Spotted Tail's Folk: A History of the Brule Sioux*. Norman: University of Oklahoma Press, 1961.

"Indigenous Languages Spoken in the United States." Available online. URL: http://www.yourdictionary.com/elr/natlang.html.

Isenberg, Andrew. *The Destruction of the Bison: An Environmental History, 1750–1920*. New York: Cambridge University Press, 2001.

Kadlecek, Edward and Mabell Kadlecek. *To Kill an Eagle: Indian Views on the Death of Crazy Horse*. Boulder, Colo.: Johnson Books, 1981.

Kilman, Carrie. "Wounded Knee: A Campaign to Rescind Medals," Teaching Tolerance, February 3, 2005. Available online. URL: http://www.tolerance.org/news/article_tol.jsp?id=1355.

Leckie, William. *The Buffalo Soldiers: A Narrative of the Negro Cavalry in the West*. Norman: University of Oklahoma Press, 1967.

Libby, O.G. *The Arikara Narrative of the Campaign Against the Hostile Dakotas, June 1876*. Mattituck, NY: J.M. Carroll, 1976 [1920].

Linderman, Frank. *Plenty-Coups: Chief of the Crows*. Lincoln: University of Nebraska Press, 1957 [1930].

Lott, Dale. *American Bison: A Natural History*. Berkeley: University of California Press, 2003.

"Man Rescued by the Eagles," Transcribed by George Bushotter. Lakota Language. Available online. URL: http://www.inext.cz/siouan/bushotter/bushotter.htm.

Marshall, Joseph III. *The Journey of Crazy Horse: A Lakota History*. New York: Viking Penguin, 2004.

Martin, Cy. *The Saga of the Buffalo*. New York: Hart Publishing, 1973.

Matthiessen, Peter. *In the Spirit of Crazy Horse*. New York: Viking Penguin, 1983.

Maurer, Evan, et al. *Visions of the People: A Pictorial History of Plains Indian Life*. Minneapolis: Institute of Arts, 1992.

McMurtry, Larry. *Crazy Horse*. New York: Penguin, 1999.

Miles, Nelson. *Personal Recollections and Observations of Nelson A. Miles*. Lincoln: University of Nebraska Press, 1992 [1896].

Moeller, Bill and Jan Moeller. *Crazy Horse: His Life, His Lands. A Photographic Biography*. Wilsonville, Ore.: Beautiful America Publishing, 1987.

Mooney, James. *The Ghost-Dance Religion and Wounded Knee*. Mineola, NY: Dover, 1991 [1896].

Murray, Robert. *The Bozeman Trail, Highway to History*. Fort Collins, Colo.: Old Army Press, 1999.

Nadeau, Remi. *Fort Laramie and the Sioux Indians*. Englewood Cliffs, NJ: Prentice-Hall, 1967.

Neihardt, John. *Black Elk Speaks: Being the Life Story of a Holy Man of the Oglala Sioux*. Lincoln: University of Nebraska Press, 1979 [1932].

Nieves, Evelyn. "On Pine Ridge, a String of Broken Promises," *Washington Post*, October 21, 2004. Available online. URL: http://www.washingtonpost.com/wp-dyn/articles/A49822-2004Oct20.html.

Paul, R. Eli. *Blue Water Creek and the First Sioux War, 1854–56*. Norman: University of Oklahoma Press, 2004.

Pearson, Jeffrey. "Nelson A. Miles, Crazy Horse, and the Battle of Wolf Mountains," *Montana: The Magazine of Western History* 51 (Winter 2001): 53–67. Available online . URL: http://visitmt.com/history/Montana_the_Magazine_of_Western_History/wolfmountain.htm.

Price, Catherine. *The Oglala People, 1841–79: A Political History.* Lincoln: University of Nebraska Press, 1996.

Reynolds, Quentin. *Custer's Last Stand.* New York: Random House, 1951.

Roberts, Chris. "Russell Means—American Indian Movement activist—Interview." *The Progressive,* September 2001. Available online. URL: http://findarticles.com/p/articles/mi_m1295/is_9_65/ai_77811474/?tag=content;col1.

Robinson, Charles, ed. *The Diaries of John Gregory Bourke.* 3 vols. Denton: University of North Texas Press, 2003–2007.

Roe, Frank. *The North American Buffalo: A Critical Study of the Species in Its Wild State.* Toronto: University of Toronto Press, 1970.

Sajna, Mike. *Crazy Horse: The Life behind the Legend.* New York: John Wiley and Sons, 2000.

Sandoz, Mari. *Crazy Horse: The Strange Man of the Oglalas.* Lincoln: University of Nebraska Press, 1942.

Schwartz, Stephanie. "The Arrogance of Ignorance: Hidden Away, Out of Sight and Out of Mind," Manataka American Indian Council, October 15, 2006. Available online URL: http://www.manataka.org/page1881.html.

Scott, Douglas, P. Willey, and Melissa Connor. *They Died with Custer: Soldiers' Bones from the Battle of the Little Bighorn.* Norman: University of Oklahoma Press, 1998.

Sklenar, Larry. *To Hell with Honor: Custer and the Little Bighorn.* Norman: University of Oklahoma Press, 2000.

Smith, Rex. *Moon of the Popping Trees: The Tragedy at Wounded Knee and the End of the Indian Wars.* Lincoln: University of Nebraska Press, 1975.

Soule, Doris. "Lieutenant Casper Collins: Fighting the Odds at Platte Bridge," *Wild West,* December 1996. Available online. URL: http://www.historynet.com/lieutenant-casper-collins-fighting-the-odds-at-platte-bridge.htm.

"Standing at the Crossroads," *Lincoln Journal Star,* June 2005. Available online. URL: http://www.journalstar.com/special_reports/whiteclay/.

Svaldi, David. *Sand Creek and the Rhetoric of Extermination: A Caste Study in Indian-White Relations.* Lanham, NY: University Press of America, 1989.

Taylor, Colin. *The Plains Indians.* New York: Crescent Books, 1994.

"Treaty with the Sioux . . . April 29, 1868," Charles Kappler, ed. *Indian Affairs: Laws and Treaties,* Vol. 2. Washington: Government Printing Office, 1904. Available online. URL: http://digital. library.okstate.edu/kappler/Vol2/treaties/sio0998.htm.

Vestal, Stanley. *Sitting Bull: Champion of the Sioux.* Norman: University of Oklahoma Press, 1989 [1932].

Walker, Carson. "Crazy Horse Memorial Turns 60 with No End in Sight," Boston.com, June 2. 2008. Available online at http://www.boston.com/news/nation/articles/2008/06/02/crazy_horse_memorial_turns_60_with_no_end_in_sight/.

Welch, James. *Killing Custer: The Battle of the Little Big Horn and the Fate of the Plains Indians.* New York: Penguin, 1995.

Williams, Florence. "Plains Sense: Frank and Deborah Popper's 'Buffalo Commons' is creeping toward reality," *High Country News*, January 15, 2001. Available online. URL: http://www. hcn.org/issues/194/10194.

"Writing Systems and Languages of the World: Sioux," Omniglot. Available online. URL: http://www.omniglot.com/writing/ sioux.htm.

FURTHER RESOURCES

Brown, Dee. *Bury My Heart at Wounded Knee*. New York: Bantam, 1971.

Blish, Helen. *A Pictographic History of the Oglala Sioux*. Lincoln: University of Nebraska Press, 1967.

Calloway, Collin, ed. *Our Hearts Fell to the Ground: Plains Indian Views of How the West Was Lost*. Boston: St. Martin's Press, 1996.

Greene, Jerome, ed. *Lakota and Cheyenne: Indian Views of the Great Sioux War, 1876–1877*. Norman: University of Oklahoma Press, 1994.

Ostler, Jeffrey. *The Plains Sioux and U.S. Colonialism from Lewis and Clark to Wounded Knee*. New York: Cambridge University Press, 2004.

Remington, Gwen. *The Sioux*. San Diego: Lucent Books, 2000.

Utley, Robert. *The Lance and the Shield: The Life and Times of Sitting Bull*. New York: Henry Holt, 1993.

Web Sites

Conversations with Crazy Horse Source Materials

http://www.astonisher.com/archives/museum/rosebud/index.html

This is a free resource for materials about Crazy Horse. It features "100 Voices," the largest and most complete collection of eyewitness accounts of the Battle of the Little Bighorn, as told by people who were there.

Dakota-Lakota Sioux Language

http://www.native-languages.org/dakota.htm

A resource for learning about the Dakota-Lakota language, including prayers, names, body parts, colors, and vocabulary.

Little Bighorn Battlefield National Monument

http://www.nps.gov/libi/

This site, created by the U.S. Department of Interior's National Park Service, showcases the place where the U.S. 7th Cavalry fought the Sioux and Cheyenne in one of the tribes' last efforts to preserve their way of life.

Midwest Archeological Center, "Archeology of the Battle of the Little Bighorn"

http://www.nps.gov/history/mwac/libi/

This site was also developed by the U.S. Department of Interior's National Park Service. It features detailed information about the Battle of the Little Bighorn and those who fought on that historic day.

New Perspectives on the West, PBS

http://www.pbs.org/weta/thewest/program/

A multimedia guide about the eight-part documentary series on the West.

Oglala Sioux Tribe at Pine Ridge Reservation

http://home.comcast.net/~zebrec/index.html

A Web site dedicated to the Oglala Sioux tribe, for those interested in the Native American way of life.

"Travel the Bozeman Trail," Fort Phil Kearney/Bozeman Trail Association

http://www.bozemantrail.org/

Sponsored by the Fort Phil Kearney/Bozeman Trail Association, this site educates readers about historic sites along the Bozeman Trail.

PICTURE CREDITS

Page

INDEX

Page numbers in *italics* indicate photos or illustrations, and page numbers followed by *m* indicate maps.

ABOUT THE AUTHOR

Jon Sterngass is the author of *First Resorts: Pursuing Pleasure at Saratoga Springs, Newport, and Coney Island* (Johns Hopkins University Press, 2001). He currently is a freelance writer specializing in children's nonfiction books. He has written more than 40 books; his most recent works are a biography of Geronimo and an analysis of the steroids controversy in the United States. Born and raised in Brooklyn, he has a B.A. in history from Franklin and Marshall College, an M.A. from the University of Wisconsin-Milwaukee in medieval history, and a Ph.D. from City University of New York in nineteenth-century American history. He has lived in Saratoga Springs, New York, for 16 years with his wife, Karen Weltman, and sons Eli (16) and Aaron (13). He has always admired Crazy Horse since reading Quentin Reynolds's "Landmark Book" biography of George Custer many years ago.